民国四川话英语教科书

英汉对照

[加] 启尔德 著

CHINESE LESSONS
for
First Year Students in West China

四川人民出版社

图书在版编目（CIP）数据

民国四川话英语教科书：英汉对照 /（加）启尔德著. —— 成都：四川人民出版社，2025.6. —— ISBN 978-7-220-11908-8

Ⅰ. H172.3

中国国家版本馆 CIP 数据核字第 20253UN628 号

MINGUO SICHUANHUA YINGYU JIAOKESHU
民国四川话英语教科书（英汉对照）
[加] 启尔德 著

责任编辑	董 玲　谢 寒
装帧设计	李其飞
责任印制	周 奇　刘雨飞
责任校对	吴 玥

出版发行	四川人民出版社（成都市锦江区三色路 238 号新华之星 A 座 33、35 层）
网　　址	http://www.scpph.com
E-mail	scrmcbs@sina.com
新浪微博	@四川人民出版社
微信公众号	四川人民出版社
发行部业务电话	(028) 86361653　86361656
防盗版举报电话	(028) 86361653
照　　排	四川胜翔数码印务设计有限公司
印　　刷	成都蜀通印务有限责任公司
成品尺寸	160mm×240mm
印　　张	18.75
字　　数	200 千
版　　次	2025 年 6 月第 1 版
印　　次	2025 年 6 月第 1 次印刷
书　　号	ISBN 978-7-220-11908-8
定　　价	52.00 元

■版权所有·侵权必究
本书若出现印装质量问题，请与我社发行部联系调换
电话：(028) 86361653

To Omal L. Kilborn

目录
CONTENTS

Chinese Lessons for First Year
Students in West China
(影印版)
001

出版后记
292

CHINESE LESSONS

for

First Year Students in West China

By

Omar L. Kilborn, M.A., M.D.

Published by the Union University

1917

CONTENTS

	Pages
INTRODUCTION	I-X

LESSONS

	Sentence
✓ 1. Conversation with the Teacher	1
2. Hiring a Cook	38
3. Hiring a Coolie	55
4. Hiring a Woman Servant	76
5. Giving the Cook his Orders	106
✓ 6. Sweeping the Floor	136
7. Washing the Floor	153
8. Dusting	178
9. Arranging the Furniture	199
10. Piling Boxes	221
11. Buying a Sedan Chair	261
12. Sedan Chair Riding	296
13. Travelling by Sedan Chair	326
14. On the Road	366
15. Changing Dollars	466
16. Changing Silver	480
17. Cleaning the Lamp	516
✓ 18. Washing Dishes	543
✓ 19. The Kitchen	565
✓ 20. Setting the Table	584
21. Putting the Food on the Table	602
22. Cooking Eggs	639
✓ 23. Cooking the Porridge	684
24. Carrying a Letter	714
25. Carrying a Lantern	734
26. Buying Firewood	769
27. Buying Coal	799
28. Washing Clothes	829
29. Ironing	876
✓ 30. The Bedroom	906
✓ 31. The Bathroom	939
32. Keeping a Cow	956

INTRODUCTION

The first business of the missionary on arrival in China is to "get the language". And most missions now allow the first two years for language study. We might better avoid that word "allow"; saying rather that a minimum of two years is *required* by most missions for language study, during which period no other responsibility is put upon the new worker. I believe that we shall soon come to the point when no new worker will be given more than partial responsibility during his third and perhaps his fourth years, so that he may have large freedom for perfecting himself in the language, and in methods and principles of work.

In the acquisition of Chinese, the ability to speak and to hear comes first in importance; much farther down in the scale comes reading; and much lower still, the ability to write Chinese characters. All four processes should be carried on together, but far the most emphasis placed on the first two, and the least emphasis on the last, at any rate in the first year. It is clear that a word or a sentence which we are able to speak and to hear, will be easily picked up in the character. To reverse the process is like the study of the dead languages.

The principle that I have had in mind in the preparation of these sentences is the supreme importance of the spoken language, as compared with the characters. I believe that we should first study *words* and *sentences*, not characters, and not even idioms. This is surely the natural order; for man learned to speak long ages before he ever thought of writing. Neither did he learn idioms first; he began to speak, and when he had learned to write his speech, he began to discover or to make order and unity, and to designate some of his peculiarities of speech as idioms.

But what words and sentences shall we study? Now life is short, especially when we are dealing with a task

II

of such herculean proportions as ours. Then why not spend a good portion of our time during our first year on the mass of words, phrases and sentences, which we are virtually compelled to learn after some fashion, whether we would or no? I mean those found in the conversations that we hold every day with servants, teachers, coal merchants, and many others,—all of whom we may adopt as our teachers of Chinese.

At any rate I have here selected a few, which are among those that we shall have to use from the beginning, and which we shall have to keep on using every year, and almost every day of our lives, so long as we live in this land. It is an effort to go straight to the point; to get at what we all need most, at least at the beginning,—a free use of everyday language, in its simplest forms.

Colloquialisms and Localisms.—An expression may be regarded as colloquial which is in use by the better classes of Chinese, regardless of its use or otherwise in books, papers or magazines. I see no reason why we should hesitate to make use of the thousands of expressions common on the lips of Chinese literary men. I well remember how one of my first teachers carefully explained to me the impropriety of the use of the vulgar words "DJER[1]" and "LER[1]" (這 and 那 as often pronounced in Chengtu); I should always say "DJE[1]" and "LA[1]", the regular dictionary pronunciation. A day or two later I had occasion to call my teacher across the courtyard; he promptly replied in a loud voice, "DZAI[4] DJER[1]"!

Undoubtedly there are many words and phrases and pronunciations in use by the most illiterate, which we would do well to avoid, especially in dignified language, as in addresses and sermons. But we shall fail dismally if we go to the opposite extreme of limiting ourselves to book words and phrases. Let us adapt our language to the circumstances and to our company; but to do this one's range of knowledge, and therefore one's experience, must be wide.

A localism is merely a word or expression or a pronunciation peculiar to a locality, usually a city and its vicinity.

The pronunciation of the characters referred to above, 這 and 那, while good colloquial here, is undoubtedly a localism. For one does not need to travel far from Chengtu before he finds that these and such words as 崽子 SHA⁴ DZ⁴, 那麼個 LA⁴ MO³ GO⁴ or LANG⁴ GO⁴, 在那根前 DZAI⁴ LA⁴ GEN¹ TSIEN² or DZAI⁴ LER¹ GEN¹ TSIEN², etc., have ceased to be used. Chungking makes 侯 HER⁴, and ends most sentences with a GO⁴. Kiating has so many localisms as to constitute almost a distinct dialect. Junghsien drops final G in all words with the romanized ending ANG, etc., etc. Now the indication is to determine for oneself just where we will draw the line. Shall we learn and use all the peculiarities of our own station? Most assuredly we are entirely at liberty to do so, if we wish. Some of us do this, and believe we are justified in so doing. Others of us again prefer to draw the line within wider limits; make the bounds of the localism coincident with those of the province, for instance, and freely accept such peculiarities as seem to be used pretty well over the province. For example 榮 is pronounced JUNG² in most other provinces, but Szechwan calls it YUIN². Certain variations prevail over a large section of the province. If we live within that section we shall probably elect to govern our language accordingly; or we may prefer to keep to the usages of other provinces, coupled with that of the half of our own province.

Chinese Teachers.—It is a good rule to regard one's teacher as the authority, in case he and the dictionary differ. But we should keep an open mind; for one's teacher should be changed at the end of the first year, and will probably be changed at longer or shorter intervals afterwards; and we soon find that teachers differ, often radically, even those who have grown up in the same city. In course of time we shall be able to form a judgment for ourselves, comparing what our teacher or teachers give us with what one or more dictionaries say.

It goes without saying that we should always treat our teachers as gentlemen, and in so doing we shall seldom be disappointed. A little tact and kindly thought go a long way. For instance, a cup of tea in the middle of the long half day of study, especially in warm weather, costs us little, and helps greatly towards a friendly relationship. It is better to have fixed hours for study with the teacher, if possible, which are arranged on engaging him; just as we arrange the exact amount of his salary. Tact should be mingled with firmness in

IV

requiring him to be punctual and regular at his work Persistence in ignoring one's wishes in these matters is best followed by dismissal, and change to another. But all this may be without engendering ill-feeling on either side. Let us remember that some of our strongest and most successful ministers of the Gospel in West China began as personal teachers. Perhaps this new man whom we have engaged may arrive at this much-to-be-desired consummation!

Dictionaries.—Begin with Baller's Analytical Vocabulary of the New Testament, and use it for all scripture reading. For this purpose there is nothing else to be compared with it. Then for daily reference use Grainger's "Western Mandarin" and Baller's or Williams' Dictionary, larger edition. I rather prefer the latter, because of its larger number of characters. The new Giles is too expensive; the difference between it and Williams is not worth the extraordinary cost. Get a Soothill for pocket use and for travelling. Add another dictionary now and again, as you have opportunity and the desire to enlarge your library. After a year or two get a Kanghsi: it is invaluable.

May I add a word on the use of the dictionary. I am firmly convinced of the value of one's own personal use of the dictionary, even Williams or Giles I mean in preference to having one's teacher turn up characters. The study of the strokes and of the parts of the character necessary in order to enable one to find it, helps greatly to fix the form and meaning in one's mind. I think we should use the dictionary constantly. Every time we happen upon an unknown character, or one that is only partially familiar, let us look it up; the result is much better than that of merely asking the teacher for sound and meaning. If the teacher is present, by all means do both; but in any case do not neglect to look it up in the dictionary. Sometimes a character seems to be peculiarly elusive; we forget sound or tone, or some aspect of its meaning, with monotonous regularity The remedy is to "look it up" with the same "monotonous regularity"; and presently we discover that that character has become a part of us,—so solidly that we never forget it again.

Tones.—The day and generation that affected to despise the tones has gone by. But that of those who

V

neglect them is still with us,—more's the pity. For the tones are just as much a part of the words as are any other part of the sounds, and Chinese without the tones, or with inaccurate tones, is broken Chinese.

Now so far as I have had opportunity for comparison with the language of other provinces, I would say that our West China tones are marked, and our spoken language is decidedly musical. It is astonishing and lamentable what one misses who fails to get the tones, and to always get them I shall venture to quote a passage from the introduction to "Lessons in Conversational Chinese", by Mr. Warren, which is most apt.—

"Remember this: you do not know a Chinese word unless you know its tone. You may reply: 'How is it that the Chinese themselves do not know the tone of a word?' The knowledge of the *name* of a tone and that of the tone itself are two different things. The Chinese do know the tone; only the educated, and indeed only the very highly educated, know the name of the tone of any particular word. For us to ask a Chinese, 'Did you say *shang-pin* or *hsia-pin*?' is very much like a Chinese asking us with regard to 'bears' and 'pears'— 'Did you use a surd or a sonant?' The majority of Englishmen would be quite unable to answer this question. But if the Chinese were able to ask us, 'Did you say "bear" or "pear"?' any Englishman would answer at once. . . . . .

"From the very first begin to train your ear to *hear* the tones. Never ask, 'What tone is that word?' Make yourself go the longer way of listening till you hear what tone it is. If you have not caught it, ask, 'Did you say ——?' and give an emphasized first, second or whichever tone you like. In this way you will stand a chance of learning to speak Chinese as the Chinese do. Any other way of learning tones simply gives you the chance of getting a good mark in answer to an examination question. Outside the answering of those questions, it is no use knowing that the Chinese word for 'Heaven' is in the first tone, and for 'Field' in the second, if when you say 'Tien' you are not conscious whether you used either or neither of these tones."

All of which I most heartily endorse. Never ask a teacher for a tone; ask him to repeat the word, again

VI

and again, if need be, until you can decide for yourself what tone it is in.

West China is supposed to have all five tones; and for many parts this is quite true. Other places—including Chengtu and Chungking have only four, for the second and fifth are synonymous. A Chengtu man finds great difficulty in distinguishing a fifth tone. I have therefore ventured to follow the language of Chengtu and Chungking, by indicating four tones only, doing away with the fifth, and placing all these under the second.

It is now generally accepted that the numbering of the tones, by the use of figures placed at the right hand upper corner of the romanized, is the quickest and easiest method. I have adopted this method. In cases where there are two tones, one used in the book language and one in the spoken, the latter is given.

Romanisation.—That which I have used is the Standard, with a few modifications to adapt it for West China. I shall not attempt to open a discussion on romanisation No one system is wholly satisfactory for all China, and in the nature of the case, no one system ever will be. The Standard system has advantages over any other, in my judgment; and if this book had been intended for more than West China, I should have adhered to it wholly. Some of the changes that I have made in it might have been better not made; or at least so I have come to think since these pages went to press

However, romanisation is to be regarded as a help during the early months of study only; it is no part of the Chinese language, and should be neglected and finally discarded, just as soon as the student can do without it. It should be suggestive only, of the sounds, not an authoritative record. The sounds must be learned from the lips of a Chinese, or of many Chinese, because we find that not all pronounce the same words alike. And so it comes to pass in time that we must use our own judgment, aided by our experience and by our dictionaries, in deciding which sound of a character we shall adopt.

Much depends upon the careful cultivation of one's ear. We cannot reproduce what we do not hear. Sometimes a new worker will spend hours in the effort to satisfy his teacher on a sound. He believes that he reproduces the sound accurately, but is really unable to catch the fine distinctions that are heard and spoken by his Chinese teacher. Unfortunately the teacher is unable to explain just what is wrong, or if he does, we do not understand him. And so in some instances the teacher gives up in despair, and allows his pupil to continue his mispronunciation. Here is one of the times where the help of a fellow-missionary is exceedingly valuable—at least it will be so if the fellow-missionary has already met and conquered the difficulty referred to. Here is one of the many advantages of the language school, or "Missionaries' Training School", such as is carried on as a department of the Union University at Chengtu.

Learning Characters.—How to do it? There is no royal road to the acquisition of Chinese characters; but some roads are better than others. Nothing else can ever take the place of dogged perseverance; it is review, and *review*, and then review again, until the characters needing review grow steadily less in number, even to the vanishing point.

I don't believe in the "pencil habit", and I hope you won't get it. I mean simply the practice of writing the romanisation, with sound and tone and meaning, whether on the margin of the study-book, or on little squares of paper. In the former instance the pencil marks detract from the direct study of the character, and they tend to a distinct neglect of effort or a weakened effort at memorisation. Similarly with the squares of paper: sound, tone and meaning are too convenient; but the biggest objection to this method is the utter lack of all connection between the characters. All the advantage of context is lost. A far better method in my experience is the following: buy three copies of John's Gospel, in large type; let your teacher use one, while you use another. After working through a few chapters, begin a review, marking all characters difficult to remember as you go along. Mark them by encircling each with a red mark, ink or pencil, but leave no indication of sound, tone or meaning. Review all marked characters daily, invariably looking up in the dictionary all characters impossible to recognize. Never be satisfied with ability to give sound and meaning only; uncertainty of tone alone is ample warrant for turning the character up in the dictionary.

VIII

By the time you have finished the Gospel, you will have marked a goodly number of characters. Then take up your clean copy and review the whole Gospel, once more marking all uncertain characters. Review the marked characters daily, until you have mastered every character in the book; that is to say, until you know every character, and you know that you know them. From that time forward, the study of characters will be perceptibly easier

What about writing characters? Use a pencil or foreign pen, and begin, as soon as you like. If you prefer the Chinese brush pen, use it If you have aptitude for character-writing, give yourself a fair chance, and you will profit greatly by the exercise. If you seem to have little or no aptitude, you will not spend much time at it, but better keep pegging away, and however slow your progress, it all helps. No character is ever known perfectly until one can write it. Let us once fix a character in our memory by writing it, and it is with us forever

I have come to think much more of late years of the value of the ability to write characters. The foreign pastor finds his influence and his usefulness greatly increased by his letters to his Chinese assistants, written with his own hand. the contents of which are therefore not public property, as is the case when a Chinese amanuensis is used. The foreign teacher gains immensely in facility and efficiency when he is able to write his texts or his syllabi on the blackboard I venture to suggest that not many foreign missionaries, no matter what the department of work, will be other than distinctly and decidedly advantaged by the ability to write even a few characters

As to the best method for learning to write,—I will only suggest that in my experience a foreign pencil does very well; and that the student should sit beside his teacher, watch him write a very few characters daily, then attempt them himself, with his teacher as critic Take particular pains to note the order of strokes; note all the minor differences between his characters and yours, as you compare after writing. Then imitate, imitate. But do not under any circumstances spend so much time at character-writing as to interfere with your regular study of the spoken language. Speech first, reading next, and last of all writing.

How to Use this Book.—The first chapter is intended mostly for reference. There has been no attempt to put easier lessons first; you are at perfect liberty to begin literally anywhere, even in the middle of a lesson, if you wish. You will find, however, that the first hundred sentences have not only the romanisation, but also complete literal translation. The second hundred have dropped the literal translation, and the two hundredth sentence is the last to have the complete romanisation. After this, also, the characters printed separately beneath are reduced in size, and are not set out so markedly, but are run together with the English comment, making solid paragraphs, and taking much less space than before.

Looking to the value of repetition, in order to facilitate study, I have not hesitated to repeat comments and explanations, even again and again. This practice will also conduce to the study of any chapter at any time.

Please do not hesitate to alter any sentence or phrase, to make it accord with the practice in your locality. I would suggest that these sentences be used to make conversation with one or another, thus securing several possible modes of expression, sometimes differing slightly in shades of meaning, or they may be identical. Compare and decide for yourself. See that the tones as I have marked them agree with yours; alter them where they differ Similarly, alter romanisations to suit your practice, or your preference. In a word, use the book in any and every possible way, so long as you derive some help from it. For this is the only reason for its existence.

Conclusion.—It is trite advice, I know, but nevertheless I will say here that "the only way to learn to speak Chinese is to speak it!" Speak with teacher, with cook and coolie and woman-servant, and with strangers. Speak with fellow-travellers on the road, with farmers in the country, with fellow-guests in inn and tea-shop. Listen carefully to their remarks; pick up what you can, if only a word from one, or a phrase from another. Make notes when convenient, and investigate on returning to your study. It is a great boon to us missionaries that the Chinese practically never laugh at our blunders in trying to learn their language.

x

Therefore even the most timid of us need feel no hesitancy in using any word, phrase or sentence that we have learned, or that we have only half learned. We will rarely meet with anything but sympathy from the Chinese in our efforts.

Never let your ears grow deaf! Always keep them open for new words and phrases; for only in this way will you not only make progress, but succeed in preventing yourself from losing ground. To stand still is to retrograde. Keep moving! Keep smiling!

OMAR L. KILBORN.

Chengtu, November, 1917.

LESSON I. 第一課

同教書先生說話
Conversation with the Teacher

同教書先生說話

√1 Conversation with the Teacher.

TUNG,² GIAO¹ SHU¹ SIEN¹ SEN¹ SHO² HWA⁴.
With teach books teacher speak words.

教書
GIAO¹ SHU¹   to teach; *lit.*, to teach books.

先生
SIEN¹ SEN¹,   teacher, mister; *lit.*, before or first born. This most common designation may now be used in addressing men—and even women teachers—in all grades of society.

說話
SHO² HWA⁴   to speak, to talk; *lit.*, to speak words.

請進來

√2 Please come in.

TSIN³ DZIN⁴ LAI².
Please enter come.

CHINESE LESSONS

請

TSIN³   please,—very much used by all classes of Chinese. In addressing the teacher, it is properly used. If, however, one is speaking to a servant, one should say simply 進來 DZIN¹ LAI², without the 'please'.

請 坐

3 Please sit down.

TSIN³ DZO⁴.   This is the proper phrase with
Please sit.   which to address teacher or guest after he has entered the room. This is also the expression one should use by way of excusing oneself, in leaving the room. As we rise to leave the room for the moment, the teacher should rise too, at least slightly. But whether he does or not, we use this expression to him.

先生這麽早

4 Good morning, Teacher.

SIEN¹ SEN¹ DJE⁴ MO³ DZAO³.
Teacher   thus   early.

不早

5 It is not early.

BU² DZAO³.   This is a modest expression, by
Not early.   way of reply to the compliment in the greeting above.

先生貴姓

6 What is your name, teacher?

SIEN¹ SEN¹ GWEI⁴ SIN⁴.
Teacher honorable name.

CONVERSATION WITH THE TEACHER

貴

GWEI[1] honorable; 姓 SIN[4], name *i.e.*, surname. There is nothing in the form of the sentence to indicate that it is interrogative; yet this particular sentence is always so. Except to a child or sometimes a coolie, the 貴 GWEI[4], honorable, should always be used.

姓張

7 My name is Djang.

SIN[4] DJANG[1]. The expression 做 姓, BI[4] SIN[4], is
Name Djang. not ordinarily used in Szechwan.

轉教

8 May I in turn ask your name?

DJWAN[3] GIAO[4]. That is to say,—"May I in turn
Turn instruct. be instructed?" which is the height of politeness, and is constantly used by all of the teacher or literary class. Note that this character to teach or instruct, is here used in its proper tone, the fourth.

姓李

9 My name is Li.

SIN[4] LI[3]. Again the entire absence of the
Name Li. self-depreciatory term 做 BI[4] or
賤 DZIEN[4] = unworthy. These terms are sometimes used by men from the country, but not at all by those in the city.

請先生在這裡坐

10 Will you please sit here.

TSIN[3] SIEN[1] SEN[1] DZAI[4] DJE[4] LI[3] DZO[4].
Please teacher here sit.

CHINESE LESSONS

請
TSIN³ please, is apt to be the opening word of the sentence, as here.

在這裡
DZAI⁴ DJE⁴ LI³, *lit.* in this inside. The whole phrase is the common expression for *here.* In Chengtu the corruption DZAI⁴ DJER¹ is much heard; or even the single word DJER¹.

這個字讀啥子

11 How is this character pronounced?
DJE⁴ GO⁴ DZ⁴ DU² SHA⁴ DZ³.
This character read what.

這
DJE⁴, with 個 GO⁴, the classifier after it = this.

那
LA⁴, with 個 GO⁴, the classifier after it = that.

字
DZ⁴ Chinese character.

啥子
SHA⁴ DZ³, the interrogative *what.* This expression is not found in Chinese books, but is good spoken language almost anywhere in West China. It is constantly heard.

讀
DU² = to study, to read. Usually with the word 書 SHU¹, book, after it, *lit.* 'study books'; commonly just = to study.

CONVERSATION WITH THE TEACHER

請再說

Please say it again.
TSIN³ DZAI⁴ SHO².
Please again say.

再
DZAI⁴ — again; much used, in all sorts of sentences.

說
SHO² — to say, to speak. 說話 SHO² HWA⁴, to speak words, to talk.
This sentence should be much used by the beginner to his teacher, in order to make absolutely sure of a tone, for instance, or of a sound. So we train our own ears to know Chinese sounds.

我說的對不對

Do I say it correctly?
NGO³ SHO² DY² DUI⁴ BU² DUI⁴.
I speak (it) correct not correct.

我
NGO³ — I, me. No change for case. Chinese is quite free from inflections, conjugations. All such matters are determined by the addition of words, or by the position of words.

的
DY² — a possessive particle, with *words*, or *sentence* understood after it. The construction is then,—The I-speak-words correct not correct? Or,—That which I speak, correct not correct?

對

14 You are speaking correctly.
    DUI⁴.
    Correct.

不對

15 You are not speaking correctly.
    BU² DUI⁴.
    Not correct.

不

BU²   not, the most common form of the
              negative.

對

DUI⁴   correct, or correctly. Whether
              adverb or adjective, it is all the
same in Chinese.

我說的不對,請先生改一下

16 If I speak incorrectly will you please correct me.
    NGO³ SHO² DY² BU² DUI¹, TSIN³ SEN¹ SIEN¹ GAI³ I² HA⁴.

I-speak-(words) not correct, please teacher change a little.
    The phrase 'NGO SHO' qualifies or possesses the word 'HWA', words, understood, after the word 'DY'; and this little possessive particle is the connecting word.
    Note that the word 'If' is understood before the pronoun 'I'. This is a very common Chinese construction. It seems awkward at first, but one soon gets quite used to it.

CONVERSATION WITH THE TEACHER

改
GAI³   change, turn, correct.

一下
I² HA⁴   'a little'. A softening phrase, placed at the end.

回回有錯,都請先生給我改一下

17 Every time I make a mistake, will you please correct me.

HWEI² HWEI² YIU³ TSO⁴, DU¹ TSIN³ SIEN¹ SEN¹ GE¹ NGO³ GAI³ I² HA⁴.

Time time have mistake, all please teacher to me correct a little.

回回
HWEI² HWEI²   time, time = every time. Very common.

有
YIU³   have; we have, you have, they have, I have, he has; also, there is, there are, there was, there were. Here it might well be translated I have, or there is.

都
DU¹   'all'. One of the many words meaning all. This is a curious idiom; it really just puts emphasis on the 回回.

給我
GE¹ NGO³   read GI² NGO³, but spoken GE¹ NGO³ = to me, for me, *e.g.* 拿給我 LA² GE¹ NGO³, bring it to me; 給給我 GE¹ GE¹ NGO³, give it to me.

這個東西叫甚麼名字

18 What is the name of this thing?
DJE⁴ GO⁴ DUNG¹ SI¹ GIAO⁴ SHEN⁴ MO³ MIN² DZ⁴.
 This   thing   called   what   name.

個
GO⁴   the most generally used classifier; it may be translated piece, this piece thing. The idiom is exactly the same as ours in pane,---this pane of glass.

東西
DUNG¹ SI¹   (*lit.*, east west) thing, article.

叫
GIAO⁴   called, to call.

甚麼
SHEN⁴ MO³   the interrogative 'what'. Much used all over China. Largely replaced in Szechwan by 晓子 SHA⁴ DZ³.

名字
MIN² DZ⁴   (*lit.*, name character), name, whether of person or thing.

請先生慢點說

19 Will you speak a little more slowly, please.
TSIN³ SIEN¹ SEN¹ MAN⁴ DIEN³ SHO².
Please teacher   slow a little speak.

CONVERSATION WITH THE TEACHER

慢 點

MAN⁴ DIEN³   (*lit.*, slow little), a little more slowly. This phrase may be used in any connection, as *e.g.*, 慢點寫 MAN⁴ DIEN³ SIE³, write a little more slowly ; 慢點念 MAN⁴ DIEN³ NIEN⁴, read a little more slowly, etc.

請先生念

20   Will you please read.

TSIN³ SIEN¹ SEN¹ NIEN⁴.

Please   teacher   read.

先 生

SIEN¹ SEN¹   may be well translated 'Mister', or even by the one word 'you', as in these last few sentences. This is an all but universal designation throughout China ; it may be used in addressing men of any station in life. Its literal meaning is "first or before born", thus showing respect to a man as though he were my elder.

請先生跟倒念

21   Will you please continue reading.

TSIN³ SIEN¹ SEN¹ GEN¹ DAO³ NIEN⁴.

Please   teacher   follow   read.

跟 倒

GEN¹ DAO³   to follow. 倒 DAO³, expresses completeness of action.

念

NIEN⁴   to read, is the most commonly used word meaning to read aloud. For reading without vocalizing, the word 看 KAN⁴, to look, to see, is used.

CHINESE LESSONS

請先生大聲說

22 Will you please read more loudly.

TSIN³ SIEN¹ SEN¹ DA⁴ SHEN¹ SHO².

Please teacher big voice speak.

大
DA⁴ big, large, great.

聲
SHEN¹ voice, sound, tone.

Lit., speak in a loud voice; but there is comparison with the present voice of the speaker, hence 'more loudly'.

請先生小聲點

23 Will you please not speak quite so loudly.

TSIN³ SIEN¹ SEN¹ SIAO³ SHEN¹ DIEN³.

Please teacher small voice little.

小
SIAO³ little, small.

點
DIEN³ a little, a point.

Note that there is no verb in this sentence. It may be used in asking the teacher not to speak or read or sing, etc., quite so loudly.

請先生慢點念

24 Will you please read a little more slowly.

TSIN³ SIEN¹ SEN¹ MAN⁴ DIEN³ NIEN¹.

Please teacher slow little read.

This is exactly similar in construction to No. 19.

CONVERSATION WITH THE TEACHER 11

請先生快點念

25 Will you please read a little more rapidly.
TSIN³ SIEN¹ SEN¹ KWAI¹ DIEN³ NIEN⁴.
Please   teacher   quick   little   read.

快

KWAI¹   quick or quickly, the opposite of
           慢 MAN⁴, slowly.

請先生念給我聽

26 Will you please read while I listen.
TSIN³ SIEN¹ SEN¹ NIEN⁴ GE¹ NGO³ TIN¹.
Please   teacher   read   for   me   listen.

我念請先生聽

27 Will you please listen while I read.
NGO³ NIEN⁴, TSIN³ SIEN¹ SEN¹ TIN¹.
I   read   please   teacher   listen.

   Note that the important words are placed first: 'I read'; then when his attention is secured, the second clause is added. There is no connecting word. The connection is plain because the two clauses are placed together.

這是常說的話嗎

28 Is this expression constantly used?
DJE⁴ SHI⁴ SHANG² SHO² DY² HWA⁴ MA¹?
This   is   constantly   spoken   word?

12 CHINESE LESSONS

This would be a simple declarative sentence, were it not for the 嗎 MA¹, at the end. The 嗎 MA¹, shows that it is interrogative. The answer to the question might well be expressed in the very same words, leaving off the 嗎 MA¹.

Note the use of the possessive particle 的 DY²; the phrase 常說 SHANG² SHO², modifies or possesses the word 話 HWA⁴. The simple sentence is 'This is word'; now put in the modifying phrase, and we have 'This is constantly-spoken-word'.

是常說的話

29 This expression is constantly used.

SHIH⁴ SHANG² SHO² DY² HWA⁴.

Is   constantly   spoken   word.

The pronoun is omitted as unnecessary; it is understood before the verb 'to be', SHIH⁴.

今天不讀書了

30 We shall not study any more today.

GIN¹ TIEN¹ BU² DU² SHU¹ LIAO³.

Today   not study books.

今天

GIN¹ TIEN¹   today.

了

LIAO³   sign of past tense ordinarily. Here it is used more as a finishing word to the sentence. It is untranslatable.

CONVERSATION WITH THE TEACHER

請先生明天來

31 Will you come tomorrow, please?
TSIN³ SIEN¹ SEN¹ MIN² TIEN¹ LAI².
Please teacher tomorrow come.

明天

MIN² TIEN¹   'tomorrow'. Look out for the tones, they are always important, but seem especially so in this word.

來

LAI²   come, to come.

This sentence may be used to dismiss the teacher for the day, without the preceding. It is polite, and unmistakable in meaning.

不讀了

32 We shall not study any longer.
BU² DU² LIAO³ This is a brief form of No. 30, and
Not study.   may be used at any time instead of that. Any one of these three sentences may be used. One of these should be used from the beginning, for another purpose,—to indicate that it is the business of the pupil to dismiss the teacher, and not *vice versa*.

請先生下午來

33 Will you please come in the afternoon.
TSIN³ SIEN¹ SEN¹ HSIA⁴ WU³ LAI².
Please teacher afternoon come.

CHINESE LESSONS

下午
HSIA[4] WU[3]   'afternoon'. 早上 DZAO[3] SHANG[1], morning.

上半天
SHANG[4] BAN[4] TIEN[1]
   'forenoon.' 晚上 WAN[3] SHANG[4], evening.

請先生天天九點鐘來

34 Will you please come at nine oclock every morning.

TSIN[3] SIEN[1] SEN[1] TIEN[1] TIEN[1] GIU[3] DIEN[3] DJUNG[1] LAI[2].

Please teacher day day nine points clock come.

天天
TIEN[1] TIEN[1]   every day; compare 回回 HWEI[2] HWEI[2], every time.

九點鐘
GIU[3] DIEN[3] DJUNG[1]
   nine points clock, nine oclock,— the common form of expression for the time by the clock.

請先生依倒鐘點來

35 Will you please come on time.

TSIN[3] SIEN[1] SEN[1] I[1] DAO[3] DJUNG[1] DIEN[3] LAI[2].

Please teacher according to clock point come.

CONVERSATION WITH THE TEACHER

依倒
I[1] DAO[3] — according to; 照到 DJAO[4] DAO[4], same meaning. This sentence often comes in useful, and may have to be resorted to many times before the object is attained.

先生漫走

36 Please walk slowly = Good Bye

SIEN[1] SEN[1] MAN[4] DZOU[3].

Teacher slow walk.

One may use 漫走漫走 MAN[4] DZOU[3], MAN[4] DZOU[3], instead of the above. Constantly used in seeing a guest out.

請坐

37 Please be seated

TSIN[3] DZO[4]   Same as No. 3. Used here by the
Please sit.   teacher as he goes out the door, or down the steps, in response to the sentence above. That is to say,—"Don't trouble to rise, please be seated".

LESSON 2. 第二課

請伙房
Hiring a Cook

請伙房

38 Hiring a cook.

TSIN³ HO³ FANG².

Invite fire room.

The same expression is used, TSIN³, in hiring teacher, cook or coolie.

火房

HO³ FANG² cook. A well-trained cook may be called a 厨子 CHU² DZ³. This term is given by the Chinese to one who is capable of preparing a feast. Do not under any circumstances use 大師傅 DA⁴ SIH¹ FU⁴. This is a term used in the down-river ports, but not at all in Szechwan.

進來

39 Come in.

DZIN⁴ LAI² Same as No. 2 except that the
Enter come. word 請 TSIN³, please, is omitted. We are *telling* the prospective cook to come in, in this sentence; in No. 2 we were *inviting* the teacher to enter. There is no caste in China, but there are classes, and we shall

HIRING A COOK

make it easier for ourselves and for the Chinese if we frankly recognize some of these things, and order our language accordingly. A good servant is often spoiled by treating him as though he were a literary man, or by using a designation that is too high for him, as *e.g.*, 大師傅 DA⁴ SIH¹ FU⁴.

貴姓、姓王

40 What is your name? My name is Wang.
GWEI⁴ SIN⁴? SIN⁴ WANG².
Honorable name? Name Wang.

Although I have retained the 貴 GWEI⁴, honorable, here, it might have been omitted, as indeed it usually is, for all servants. No. 57 may be used. The cook is distinctly a better class servant than the coolie, and so may perhaps be allowed the 貴 GWEI⁴.

給外國人煮過飯、沒有

41 Have you ever cooked for foreigners?
GE¹ WAI⁴ GWEH² REN² DJU³ GO⁴ FAN⁴, MUH² YIU³?
For foreigners cooked food (rice), not?

外國人
WAI⁴ GWEH² REN²
Lit. 'outside country men', foreigners.

煮
DJU³ to boil, to cook.

過
GO⁴ sign of past tense.

飯
FAN¹　　　　　rice, food.

没有
MUH² YIU³　　'not have'. This phrase is exceedingly common, indicating an interrogative.

煮過
42　Yes, I have.

DJU³ GO⁴.　　This word 煮 DJU³, to boil, is
Cooked.　　　used in the more general sense
　　　　　　　of 'to cook'; just as the word 飯
FAN⁴, meaning primarily 'rice', is also used in the general sense of food.

帮過那一個
43　For whom have you worked?

BANG¹ GO⁴ LA³ I² GO⁴?

Helped　　whom?

帮
BANG¹　　　　to help, to work for; 帮過 BANG¹ GO⁴, helped.

帮忙
BANG¹ MANG²　same meaning, to help, but made into two syllables. Chinese spoken language tends to be dissyllabic.

那一個
LA³ I² GO⁴　　who, whom, with the character 那 LA³, in third tone; that, that thing, or that person, when 那 LA⁴, is in the fourth tone.

HIRING A COOK

幫過成都的李先生

44 I have worked for Mr. Li of Chengtu.
BANG[1] GO[4] CHEN[2] DU[1] DY[2] LI[3] SIEN[1] SEN[1].
Helped   Chengtu   Mr. Li.

Lit., 'Helped Mr. Li'. What Mr. Li? 'The Chengtu Mr. Li'. The two characters 成都 CHENGTU, are a phrase modifying the phrase 李先生 LI[3] SIEN[1] SEN[1]. The little particle 的 DY[2], in between, indicates this modification or possession.

幫過他好久

45 How long have you worked for him?
BANG[1] GO[4] TA[1] HAO[3] GIU[3] ?
Helped him how long ?

他

TA[1]   he, she, him, her; rarely, it.

好久

HAO[3] GIU[3]   *lit.,* good long, *i.e.,* long time. In some mysterious way the character 好 HAO[3], here is translated by the English word 'how', of exactly the same sound.

幫過他兩年

46 I have worked for him for two years.
BANG[1] GO[4] TA[1] LIANG[3] NIEN[2].
Helped   him   two   years.

要好多錢一個月

47 How much do you want per month?

YAO⁴ HAO³ DO¹ TSIEN² I² GO⁴ YUEH²?

Want how much money one (piece) month?

好多

HAO³ DO¹   how much; same construction as in No. 45. Similarly 好大 HAO³ DA⁴ how large; 好寬 HAO³ KWAN¹, how wide; 好重 HAO³ DJUNG⁴, how heavy, etc., all interrogative.

錢

TSIEN²   money, cash, wealth.

月

YUEH²   moon, month.

一個月

I² GO⁴ YUEH²   one month, *i.e.*, per month.

每月要四塊錢，吃先生的飯

48 I want four dollars a month in addition to my board.

MEI³ YUEH² YAO⁴ SIH¹ KWAI³ TSIEN², CHʼIH² SIEN¹ SEN¹ DY² FAN⁴.

Each month want four pieces money, eat your (Teacher's) food.

每

MEI³   each, every.

HIRING A COOK

一塊錢

I[2] KWAI[3] TSIEN[2] or 一元 I[2] YUEN[2], = $1.00; *lit.,* 'one piece money'. This proposal is entirely in accord with the usual custom among the Chinese, that is, for servants to get a certain wage, and their board in addition. The employer provides food for his servants and his own family, perhaps all cooked in the one pan.

我拿五塊錢,吃你自己

49 I will give you five dollars, and you provide your own food.

NGO[3] LA[2] WU[3] KWAI[3] TSIEN[2], CHÏH[2] NI[3] DZ[1] GI[3].

I bring five pieces money eat yourself.

我拿

NGO[3] LA[2]   *lit.,* I bring, I will give; constantly used in just this sense.

吃你自己

CHÏH[2] NI[3] DZ[4] GI[3]   a very expressive phrase, not at all ambiguous. It is not necessary to place the word 'you' before 'eat'; it could not be anyone else.

使得,那一天來

50 All right. What day shall I come?

SHÏH[3] DEH[2]. LA[3] I[2] TIEN[1] LAI[2]?

Use can. What day come?

使得

SHÏH[3] DEH[2]   a very much used phrase, 'all right, that will do'. Note the tone of the 那 LA[3]. Third tone for interrogative, fourth tone when it means *that.*

明天一早來

51 Come early to-morrow morning.
MIN² TIEN¹ I² DZAO³ LAI².
To-morrow one-early come.

一早

I² DZAO³ early, really *very early*. It is emphatic.

老王,還有一句話

52 Lao Wang, I have another word to say to you.
LAO³ WANG², HAI² YIU³ I² GŬ⁴ HWA⁴.
Old Wang, yet have one sentence.

老王

LAO³ WANG² *lit.*, "Old" Wang; the usual form of address to a coolie or cook by the Chinese. It may well be used by missionaries for cook and coolie on first engaging them; to be replaced later on, after a few weeks or months, in case they prove satisfactory servants, and likely to be permanent, by the three characters of name and surname. See No. 108.

還

HAI² usually, in speech; HWAN², as usually *read* by the Chinese literary man. It is, however, spoken HWAN² in certain connections.

句

GŬ⁴ the classifier for words or sentence.

HIRING A COOK

要把鋪盖抱來,在我們這裡歇

53 You must bring your pugai and live on the premises.

YAO⁴ BA³ PU¹ GAI⁴ BAO⁴ LAI² DZAI⁴ NGO³ MEN² DJE⁴ LI³ HSIE².

Want take "pugai", carry come, at us here sleep.

把

BA³   to take; note this very characteristic construction of a sentence in Chinese. Instead of saying "Bring your pugai", they break the sentence into two shorter phrases, "Take your pugai, bring it". Make your Chinese sentences short!

鋪盖

PU¹ GAI⁴   PU¹ to spread, and GAI⁴, to cover: the ordinary thick quilt which constitutes the bedding of the masses of the people. Foreigners have practically adopted this word, because we have no word that quite expresses the meaning.

好,要抱來

54 All right; I'll bring it.

HAO³ ; YAO⁴ BAO⁴ LAI².

Good; will carry come.

抱

BAO⁴   to carry in the arms, as a quilt, a small box, or a baby.

抱 來
BAO¹ LAI²˙   to bring in the arms.

在 我 們 這 裡
DZAI⁴ NGO³ MEN² DJE⁴ LI³

Note that the three character phrase 在 這 裡 DZAI⁴ DJE⁴ LI³, is separated, and the pronoun 我 們 NGO³ MEN², us, we, inserted between the parts; here, with us; *i e.*, here at our house.

歇
HSIE²   to rest, to stay over night, to stay at night.

LESSON 3. 第三課

請打雜
Hiring a Coolie

請打雜

55　Hiring a coolie.
TSIN³ DA³ DZA².
Invite strike mixture.

打

DA³　　　　　to strike, to beat. An exceedingly common word, used in all sorts of phrases, as 打水 DA³ SHUI³, to draw water; 打油 DA³ YIU², to buy oil; 打魚 DA³ YÜ², to fish; 打雷 DA³ LUI², to thunder.

雜

DZA²　　　　a mixture, mixed. Hence the coolie who does all kinds of work is a 打雜 DA³ DZA², or 打雜的 DA³ DZA² DY².

進來

56　Come in.
DZIN⁴ LAI².

姓啥子

OR 你姓啥 NI³ SIN⁴ SHA⁴!

57 What is your name?
SIN⁴ SHA⁴ DZ³?
Surname what?

啥子

SHA⁴ DZ³ mentioned under No. 18, a very common localism in Szechwan. It is not by any means confined to the uneducated; all sorts of people use these familiar expressions. And yet they are not always suitable in the pulpit, for instance.

啥子事

SHA⁴ DZ³ SI⁴   What is all the row about?

啥子話

SHA⁴ DZ³ HWA⁴ What are you saying? This expression is used both to indicate lack of understanding of what is being said, and also on occasion to show disapproval of a remark that is understood.

姓趙

58 My name is Djao.
SIN⁴ DJAO⁴.
See note under No. 7.

哪子名字

59 What is your given name?

SHA⁴ DZ³ MIN² DZĬ⁴?

What name? (*i.e.*, 'given name')

    On learning the given name of two characters, one proceeds to call the servant by his three characters, surname first, followed by given name. This is quite proper for any man-servant. This shows more respect to him than the use of 老 LAO³. Some use the surname followed by 師 SĬ¹, but this is better avoided; it puts him too high. This is the term constantly used by one servant in addressing another. Other people's servants may be appropriately addressed as "WANG SĬ", "LI SĬ", etc. DA⁴ SĬ¹ FU⁴, should NEVER be used for the cook.

趙興順

60 My whole name is Djao Hsin Shwen

DJAO⁴ HSIN¹ SHWEN⁴.

    Instead of simply repeating his given name, as asked, he repeats the three characters of his name and surname together, in characteristic Chinese fashion. We shall call him Djao Hsin-Shwen in future lessons.

在那裡坐

61 Where do you live?

DZAI⁴ LA³ LI⁵ DZO⁴

Where   sit, (*i.e.*, live)?

坐

DZO⁴, *lit.*, to sit, but constantly used for 'dwell'.

在南門上

62　At the South Gate.

　　Dzai⁴ Lan² Men² Shang⁴.

　　　At　south gate　　on.

　　　This means anywhere in the vicinity of the south gate of the city, and is about as definite an answer as one usually gets or, perhaps, expects.

給外國人打過雜,沒有

63　Have you ever acted as coolie for foreigners?

　　Ge¹ Wai⁴ Gweh² Ren² Da³ Go⁴ Dza², Muh² Yiu³?

　　For outside country men beaten mixture, (or) not?

打過雜

　　Da³ Go⁴ Dza²　acted as coolie; 過 Go⁴, sign of past tense.

沒有

64　No, I have not.

　　Muh² Yiu³.

　　Not have.

　　　Compare 不是的 Bu² Shï⁴ Dy², no, it is not. It is clear that this latter phrase would be quite inappropriate here.

要現學

65　You will have to learn (from the beginning).

　　Yao⁴ Hsien⁴ Hsioh².

　　Must　now　　learn.

HIRING A COOLIE

現
HSIEN⁴ — part of the very common word 現在 HSIEN⁴ DZAI⁴, one of the most common translations of the little word 'now'. This character is constantly spoken "SÜEN⁴", and has the sense given in the translation above 'from the beginning'.

耍掃地、洗地、撇灰

66 You will be required to sweep, wash floors and dust.

YAO⁴ SAO³ DI⁴, SI³ DI⁴, MA² HWEI¹.

Want sweep ground, wash ground, wipe dust.

掃
SAO³ — to sweep; 掃把 SAO⁴ BA³, a broom; note change of tone.

地
DI⁴ — *lit.*, ground, but constantly used for floor.

撇
MA² — properly MO¹, but here read MA², to wipe, as in dusting.

灰
HWEI¹ — dust; 灰塵 HWEI¹ CHEN², the complete word for dust.

地板
DI⁴ BAN³ — floor boards; 地陳 DI⁴ DJEN⁴ or 地陳板 DI⁴ DJEN⁴ BAN³, complete words for floor.

擔水，擔得嗎

67 Can you carry water (with shoulder pole)?

DAN¹ SHUI³, DAN¹ DEH² MA¹?

Carry water, carry can?

擔
DAN¹   to carry with shoulder pole. 挑 TIAO¹, exactly the same.

擔子
DAN⁴ DZ³   a man-load as so carried. Note change of tone.

嗎
MA¹   note change of tone to the first here. Constantly so changed for euphony.

擔得

68 Yes, I can carry water.

DAN¹ DEH².

Carry can.   That is, I am able to carry.

不論甚麼時候喊做咪子，就要做咪子

69 No matter at what time you are called to do anything, you are to do it.

BU² LEN⁴ SHEN⁴ MO³ SHIH² HOU⁴ HAN³ DZU⁴ SHA⁴ DZ³, DZIU⁴ YAO⁴ DZU⁴ SHA⁴ DZ³.

Not discuss what time call anything, then want do anything.

HIRING A COOLIE

不論
BU² LEN⁴   a very common phrase meaning, 'It is matter of indifference', 'I do not care', etc.

甚麼時候
SHEN⁴ MO³ SHIH² HOU⁴; still more colloquial, 脒時候 SHA⁴ SHIH² HOU⁴.

要得

70   All right.

YAO⁴ DEH².   Do can. Or in expressive pidgin English, 'Can do'. This is a much used phrase, and very expressive, as is also its negative, 要不得 YAO⁴ BU² DEH², that will not do at all, it is very bad, etc.

趙興順,有一句要緊的話

71   Djao Hsin-Shwen, I have an important word to say to you.

DJAO⁴ HSIN¹ SHWEN⁴ YIU³ I² GŬ⁴ YAO⁴ GIN³ DY² HWA⁴.

Djao Hsin Shwen there is an important sentence.

一句話
I¹ GŬ⁴ HWA⁴,   a sentence, a remark.

要緊
YAO⁴ GIN³   'important'. This word modifies the word 話 HWA⁴, as indicated by the possessive particle 的 DY².

It is true that this sentence does not state clearly who is going to make the important remark; but nevertheless there can scarcely be any ambiguity.

來幫我們的時侯,手脚要乾淨

72 If (or when) you come to work for us, you must not pilfer.

LAI² BANG¹ NGO³ MEN² DY² SHĪ² HOU⁴, SHOU³ GIOH² YAO⁴ GAN¹ DZIN⁴.

帮助

BANG¹ DZU⁴   the full word meaning to help, here cut down to one syllable or character.

的候時

DY² SHĪ² HOU⁴, best translated by the relative 'when'; a much used and useful phrase.

手脚乾淨

SHOU³ GIOH² GAN¹ DZIN⁴.
A very expressive phrase, much used with this meaning, honest, no thieving, no pilfering.

先生放心

73 You, sir, may rest easy (on this point).

SIEN¹ SEN¹ FANG⁴ SIN¹.

Teacher   place heart.
Or as it is sometimes translated, 'Let your heart down'. A very common expression, used to reassure one under any uncertain or distressing circumstances

HIRING A COOLIE

有徐掌櫃舉荐我

74 Mr. Hsü recommends me.

YIU³ HSÜ² DJANG³ GWEI⁴ GÜ³ GIEN⁴ NGO³.

There is Hsü Proprietor recommends me.

掌櫃

DJANG³ GWEI⁴, proprietor of a shop, and used as a form of direct address in Chengtu. Elsewhere mostly 老板 LAO³ BAN³.

舉荐

GÜ³ GIEN⁴ to recommend. This always includes the taking of more or less responsibility for the character of the one recommended, by the one who does the recommending. Hence this statement by the prospective coolie. He understands that you are well acquainted with Mr. Hsü, and will be satisfied with his recommend.

好、明天來動手

75 Very good; come to-morrow to begin.

HAO³ ; MIN² TIEN¹ LAI² DUNG⁴ SHOU³.

Good; to-morrow come move hand.

動手

DUNG⁴ SHOU³ *lit.*, move hand, to begin, to commence.

LESSON 4. 第 四 課

請 老 婆 子
Hiring a Woman Servant

請 老 婆 子

76 Hiring a woman servant.
TSIN³ LAO³ PO² DZ³.

Invite (old) woman.

老 婆 子
LAO³ PO² DZ³   lit., old woman, a general term used for women of the working classes. If she is under forty the woman servant should be addressed as 'Yang Sao', 'Li Sao', etc. If over forty she may be called 'Yang Da Niang', Li Da Niang'.

要請一個老婆子洗衣裳

77 I want to hire a woman to wash clothes.
YAO⁴ TSIN³ I² GO⁴ LAO³ PO² DZ³ SI³ I¹ SHANG².
Want invite   a   woman   wash clothes.

衣 裳
I¹ SHANG²   the commonest word for clothes.
衣服 I¹ FU², clothes, also much used.

HIRING A WOMAN SERVANT

先生幫我找一個好人，
找得倒嗎、找不倒

78 Can you help me to find a good woman? (*lit.*, person).

SIEN¹ SEN¹ BANG¹ NGO³ DJAO³ I² GO⁴ HAO³ REN². DJAO³ DEH² DAO³ MA¹, DJAO³ BU² DAO³?

Teacher help me find a good person, can find (or) not find?

找

DJAO³   to find, to search.

找得倒嗎、找不倒

DJAO³ DEH² DAO³ MA¹, DJAO³ BU² DAO³

can you find (it, her, him, etc.,) or not?

好人

HAO³ REN²   good person, *i.e.* a good servant woman.

找得倒

79 I can find you a good woman.

DJAO³ DEH² DAO³.

Find can complete.

得倒

DEH³ DAO³   expresses completion of the action.

我明天舉荐一個來

80 I shall recommend one to you to-morrow.
NGO³ MIN² TIEN¹ GÜ³ GIEN⁴ I² GO⁴ LAI².
I   to-morrow recommend   one come.

老婆子來了

81 The woman arrives.
LAO³ PO² DZ³ LAI² LIAO³.
Woman   has come.

喊他進來

82 Call her in.
HAN³ TA¹ DZIN⁴ LAI².
Call her enter come.

喊他

HAN³ TA¹   to be used of servants, not of a teacher.

你貴姓

83 What is your name?
NI³ GWEI⁴ SIN⁴?
You honorable name?

Note that the character 你 NI³, is applicable to servants only. One need never be afraid to use it in addressing servants, and yet it is often used by beginners much more frequently than is necessary.

Although you are addressing a servant here yet the phrase 貴姓 GWEI⁴ SIN⁴ is quite permissable.

HIRING A WOMAN SERVANT

我姓楊

84 My name is Yang.
   NGO³ SIN⁴ YANG².
      I   name Yang.
      The 我 NGO³, may or may not be used in her reply.

在那裡坐

85 Where do you live?
   DZAI⁴ LA³ LI³ DZO⁴?
      Where   dwell?

在北門上銅絲街坐

86 On the Brass Wire Street, near the North Gate.
   DZAI⁴ BE² MEN² SHANG⁴, TUNG² SÏ¹ GAI¹ DZO⁴.
   At North Gate, Brass Wire Street sit (or dwell).

在北門上

DZAI⁴ BE² MEN² SHANG⁴
      Lit., on the North Gate. This expression is constantly used of a large section of the city in the vicinity of the North Gate.

幫過外國人沒有

87 Have you ever worked for foreigners?
   BANG¹ GO⁴ WAI⁴ GWE² REN² MU² YIU³?
      Helped   foreigners   not?

沒有帮過

88 I have never worked for (foreigners).
MU² YIU³ BANG¹ GO⁴.
  Not   helped.

有多少活路要現學

89 There is much work that you will have to learn for the first time.
YIU³ DO¹ SHAO³ HO² LU⁴ YAO⁴ SŬEN¹ HSIO².
There is much work want for the first time learn.

多少
DO¹ SHAO³   'much'; also used in the interrogative,—'how much?' but not so common as 好多 HAO³ DO¹, how much?

活路
HO² LU⁴   *Lit.*, 'living road', work; practically limited to manual labor; common.

現
HSIEN⁴   but in this sense pronounced SŬEN⁴, and meaning 'for the first time', or 'from the beginning'.

先生師母給我說，我就曉得

90 (If) Master and Mistress (will) tell me, then I will know.
SIEN¹ SEN¹ SĬ¹ MU³ GE¹ NGO³ SHO², NGO³ DZIU⁴ HSIAO³ DE².
Teacher (or Mr.) Mrs. to me say, I then know.

HIRING A WOMAN SERVANT

給我說
GE¹ NGO³ SHO², tell me. 告訴我 GAO⁴ SU⁴ NGO³ tell me, is the proper expression for the eastern provinces, but is not used in Szechwan. Better not spend time and energy trying to introduce it.

活路大約就是洗衣裳
91 Your work will be chiefly that of washing.

HO² LU⁴ DA⁴ YO² DZIU⁴ SHI⁴ SI³ I¹ SHANG².

Work chiefly (or probably) then is wash clothes.

大約
DA⁴ YO²   chiefly, for the most part; very common.

衣裳
I¹ SHANG²   clothes. Also 衣服 I¹ FU², the same; equally used.

熨衣裳、理床鋪、掃地、撏灰
92 Ironing clothes, making beds, sweeping (and) dusting.

YUIN⁴ I¹ SHANG², LI³ CHWANG² PU¹, SAO³ DI⁴, MA² HWEI¹.

Iron clothes, set in order bedding, sweep ground, wipe dust.

理床鋪
LI³ CHWANG² PU¹

Lit., set in order bed bedding. Often cut short by omitting the last character, 理床 set in order beds, *i.e.* make beds.

掃 地

SAO³ DI₄   *Lit.*, 'sweep ground', sweep floors.

撽

MA²   to wipe. This character is read MO¹ but spoken MA².

這 宗 活 路，你 肯 不 肯 做

93 Are you willing to do this kind of work?

DJE⁴ DZUNG¹ HO² LU⁴ NI³ KEN³ BU² KEN³ DZU⁴?

    This kind work you willing not willing do?

宗

DZUNG¹   sort, kind; the classifier here for 活 路 HO² LU⁴.

那 有 不 肯 做

94 Who would be unwilling to do it!

LA³ YIU³ BU² KEN³ DZU⁴!

Where are those (who would be) unwilling to do (such work)!

    This exclamatory sentence expresses the utter absence of any possible unwillingness.

師 母 喊 做 哪 子，就 做 哪 子

95 Whatever you tell me to do I will do.

SI¹ MU³ HAN³ DZU⁴ SHA⁴ DZ³, DZIU¹ DZU⁴ SHA⁴ DZ³.

Mrs. call do what, then do what.

HIRING A WOMAN SERVANT

喊
HAN³ to call, to tell, as from superior to inferior. The 咗 子 SHA⁴ DZ³, repeated might be translated 'whatever...that', *whatever* the Mistress tells me to do, *that* I will do.

楊嫂、要好多錢一個月

96 Mrs. Yang, how much to you want per month?

YANG² SAO³, YAO⁴ HAO³ DO¹ TSIEN² I² GO⁴ YUE² ?

Yang Mrs., want how much money one month?

嫂
SAO³ the best designation for a woman servant up to forty years of age. Over forty, better call her 楊大娘 YANG² DA⁴ NIANG².

一個月
I² GO⁴ YUE² one month, per month.

隨便師母給錢、就是咯

97 As you please about the pay, and I shall be satisfied.

SUI² BIEN⁴ SI¹ MU³ GE¹ TSIEN², DZIU⁴ SHI⁴ LO².

Follow convenience Mrs. give money, then all right.

隨便
SUI² BIEN⁴ as you please; much used.

給錢
GE¹ TSIEN² to give or pay money.

就是咯

DZIU⁴ SHĬ⁴ LO², and that will do; that is all there is about it.

The servant never addresses his master or mistress by the second personal pronoun 你 NI³. That would be rude. Sometimes they use it especially with the new missionary, thinking that they will go uncorrected.

可以來做倒一下

98 You may come and work for a while.

KO³ I³ LAI² DZU⁴ DAO³ I² HA⁴.

May come (and) work away for a while.

The use of the 可以 KO³ I³, softens the order or request greatly.

做倒

DZU⁴ DAO³   to do definite work.

一下

I² HA⁴   a while, for a little.

過一二十天,再說工錢

99 After ten or twenty days we shall again talk about wages.

GO¹ I² IR⁴ SHĬ² TIEN¹, DZAI⁴ SHO² GUNG¹ TSIEN².

Pass over one (ten), two tens days, again speak (about) labor money.

The number of days intended to be expressed is 'from ten to twenty days'. But the expression is not definite, it might be even over the twenty.

HIRING A WOMAN SERVANT

你有鋪蓋沒得

100 Have you bedding?
NI³ YIU³ PU¹ GAI⁴ MU² DE² ?
You have pugai not?

鋪蓋
PU¹ GAI⁴   PU¹, to spread, and GAI⁴ to cover.

有鋪蓋

101 Yes, I have bedding.
YIU³ PU¹ GAI⁴.

要把鋪蓋抱來, 在堂裏頭歇

102 You must bring your bedding and lodge on the premises. *Lit.*, in the compound.
YAO⁴ BA³ PU¹ GAI⁴ BAO⁴ LAI², DZAI⁴ TANG³ LI³ TOU² HSIE².

要
YAO⁴   in this connection, 'I want'; 'it is required'.

抱來
BAO⁴ LAI²   carry in arms come; to bring by carrying in the arms.

歇
HSIE²   to lodge, to sleep, to rest, to stay.

堂
TANG² that is the 福音堂 FU² YIN¹ TANG². We used to regard all Mission premises as Fu Yin Tang, but now the term is almost restricted to a church or chapel.

啥時候來動手

103 When shall I come to begin work?
SHA⁴ SHĬ² HOU⁴ LAI² DUNG⁴ SHOU³?

啥候時
SHA⁴ SHĬ² HOU⁴ corrupted from 甚麽時候 SHEN¹ MO³ SHĬ² HOU⁴.

動手
DUNG⁴ SHOU³ See No. 75.

我明早晨來, 使得麽

104 I shall come to-morrow morning, will that do?
NGO³ MIN² DZAO³ SHEN² LAI², SHĬ³ DE² MO¹?

明早晨
MIN² DZAO³ SHEN² or 明早上 MIN² DZAO³ SHANG,⁴ equally used.

使得
SHĬ³ DE² *Lit.*, use can; that is, can do; but with the interrogative particle 麽 MO¹ or 嗎 MA¹, it is clear that the meaning is,—'Will that do?'

These final interrogative particles 麽 MO¹ 嗎 MA¹ are usually in a high tone, 1st or 3rd; but they may fall into almost any tone, for euphony's sake.

HIRING A WOMAN SERVANT

要得,明早晨來

105 That will be satisfactory; come to-morrow morning.

YAO¹ DE² ; MIN² DZAO³ SHEN² LAI².

Unfortunately the Chinese are only beginning to punctuate. Polished Chinese is supposed to be spoiled by the introduction of even one punctuation mark. Nevertheless the newspapers are steadily using a little punctuation, and the New Testament in its latest version has a great deal.

LESSON 5. 第五課

喊伙房買東西

Giving the Cook His Orders to Buy Things

喊伙房買東西

106 Giving the cook his orders to buy things.
HAN³ HO³ FANG² MAI³ DUNG¹ SI¹.

伙房

HO³ FANG²   the most generally used term for cook in Szechwan.

買

MAI³   to buy; 賣 MAI⁴ to sell; 買賣 MAI³ MAI⁴, business, usually used for business on a small scale.

東西

DUNG¹ SI¹   lit., east west; things. Constantly used for unclassified articles, exactly like the English word 'things'. Better never use the word 東西 DUNG¹ SI¹, to or of a person; so used it expresses supreme contempt. See No. 38.

GIVING THE COOK HIS ORDERS

喊老王來

107　Call Lao Wang to come.

HAN³ LAO³ WANG² LAI².

　　We have not previously asked his given name or 名字 MIN² DZĪ¹, therefore we call him for the present 老王 LAO³ WANG². But this form of address is best reserved for the new coolie especially if he is a coarse, uneducated man. Therefore in No. 108 we proceed to get the cook's given name.

老王，你叫隊子名字

108　Lao Wang, what is your given name?

LAO³ WANG², NI³ GIAO⁴ SHA⁴ DZ³ MIN² DZĪ¹?

　　This is not a disrespectful question to ask any servant. On the contrary he usually feels rather pleased because you take this interest in him.

我叫王長興

109　I am called Wang Chang-Hsin.

NGO³ GIAO⁴ WANG² CHANG² HSIN¹.

　　See No. 59.

王長興，我要你上街買東西

110　Wang Chang-Hsin, I want you to go on the street to buy things.

WANG² CHANG² HSIN¹, NGO⁵ YAO⁴ NI³ SHANG⁴ GAI¹ MAI⁵ DUNG¹ SI¹.

上街

SHANG⁴ GAI¹   to go on the street. It may have a 去 CHÜ⁴ added, becoming 上街去 SHANG⁴ GAI¹ CHÜ⁴.

要買柴、炭、灰麵、鷄蛋、鹽

111   I want you to buy firewood, coal, flour, eggs and salt.

YAO⁴ MAI³ CHAI², TAN⁴, HWEI¹ MIEN⁴, GI¹ DAN⁴, YEN².

Note the absence of any personal pronoun at the beginning. It might be "I want" or "You are required to", or both. Perhaps a comprehensive translation would be, "It is required to buy, etc.," which covers both parties concerned. Note also the absence of any word corresponding to our 'and'. Still the Chinese constantly use the little word 給 GE¹, for 'and', where it is specially needed.

鷄蛋

GI¹ DAN⁴   hen's eggs. The 蛋 DAN⁴ may be used without the 鷄 GI¹.

請問、先生、一樣買好多

112   Will you please tell me how much I am to buy of each?

TSIN³ WEN⁴, SIEN¹ SEN¹, I² YANG⁴ MAI³ HAO³ DO¹?

GIVING THE COOK HIS ORDERS

請問
TSIN³ WEN⁴ — *lit.*, please ask; a most useful phrase to be used by the missionary in asking one's way on the street, for instance; or in asking for any information from a teacher, a guest or a stranger, but not when asking a servant something. These two characters are always placed at the beginning.

一樣
I² YANG⁴ — one kind or sort, *i.e.* (of) each kind.

好多
HAO³ DO¹ — how much or how many; the most common phrase in use in West China having this meaning.

柴可以買兩捆,炭一千斤

113 You may buy two bundles of firewood and one thousand catties of coal.

CHAI² KO³ I³ MAI³ LIANG³ KWEN³, TAN⁴ I² TSIEN¹ GIN¹.

柴
CHAI² — firewood, usually done up in bundles.

可以
KO³ I³ — may, with 'you' understood. The use of this phrase greatly softens the order.

两捆

LIANG³ KWEN³, two bundles.

Note the peculiar idiom: the noun comes first, and what is to be said or done about it, afterwards. This is an extremely important idiom, and should be carefully noted. Put the important word in the sentence first; that is the article or the question being discussed, and at once the subject of conversation is clear.

灰麵稱十斤,鷄蛋揀二十個

114 Buy ten catties of flour, and twenty eggs.

HWEI¹ MIEN⁴ CHEN¹ SHĪ² GIN¹, GI¹ DAN⁴ GIEN³ ER⁴ SHĪ² GO⁴.

Here again the nouns come first. Note the special terms used for the purchase of various articles. The Chinese do not use 'buy' for everything; *e.g.*, flour is 'weighed', 稱 CHEN¹; and eggs are 'selected'. 揀 GIEN³. These have exactly the force of 'to buy' in these cases. It is not at all impossible to use the word 買 MAI³, for all kinds of articles; but the use of these special words is much more apt, and therefore causes one to be more readily understood.

鹽可以稱一斤,就夠了

115 If you buy a catty of salt that will be enough.

YEN² KO³ I³ CHEN¹ I² GIN¹, DZIU⁴ GOU⁴ LIAO³.

就夠了

DZIU⁴ GOU⁴ LIAO³

'then enough'. 了 LIAO³, is by way of a finishing-off word. It often indicates past tense, but not here.

GIVING THE COOK HIS ORDERS

要買一個筐筐,是不是

116 I shall need to buy a basket, shall I not?
YAO⁴ MAI³ I² GO⁴ KWANG¹ KWANG¹, SHĪ⁴ BU² SHĪ⁴?

筐筐
KWANG¹ KWANG¹, a more or less general word for basket.

是不是
SHĪ⁴ BU² SHĪ⁴ lit., 'is not is', is it not, are they not, will I not, etc. In constant use, but corrupted in pronunciation most commonly to SHĪ⁴ BU² SA². There are many variations of the sounds heard for this little phrase, some of them unintelligible at first.

是的,可以買一個提篼

117 Yes, you may buy a market basket.
SHĪ⁴ DY², KO³ I³ MAI³ I² GO⁴ TI² DOU¹.

是的
SHĪ⁴ DY²   'yes'. This is the one word with this meaning, but not so frequently used, because of the Chinese habit of repeating the phrase used in asking the question, by way of affirmative answer.

提篼
TI² DOU¹   a long basket, with a handle by which it is easily carried on the arm or in the hand.

明天還要買幾樣

118 To-morrow I want you to buy several other things.
MIN² TIEN¹ HAI² YAO⁴ MAI³ GI³ YANG⁴.

明 天

MIN[2] TIEN[1]　　to-morrow; 後 天 HOU[4] TIEN[1], day after to-morrow; 昨 天 DZO[2] TIEN[1], yesterday, 今 天 GIN[1] TIEN[1], to-day; 前 天 TSIEN[2] TIEN[1], day before yesterday.

幾 樣

GI[3] YANG[4]　　several sorts or kinds Now this little word 幾 GI[3], is constantly used in the interrogative sense, as well as declarative. The sentence would be equally correct if translated, 'How many kinds of things do you want me to buy to-morrow?' You distinguish by noting who makes the remark, of course, whether master or servant. 幾 GI[3], then means 'How many', and usually refers to small numbers, most commonly under ten

水缸一個、洋芋十斤

119　A water crock (or jar) and ten catties of potatoes. SHUI[3] GANG[1] I[2] GO[1], YANG[2] YŬ[4] SHI[2] GIN[1].

水 缸

SHUI[3] GANG[1]　　water jar, which is a perfectly good English word, entirely suitable to apply to the vessel so much used in China. And, therefore, the frequent use of the Chinese word 缸 GANG[1], (often corrupted to 'gong') when speaking English, becomes inexcusable. I once heard a good missionary, upon whom this habit had become fixed, argue that 'gong' was a real English word for jar!

洋 芋

YANG[2] YŬ[1]　　lit., foreign potatoes. 山 芋 SHAN[1] YŬ[4], is a better name, but the former is pretty well fixed by usage

GIVING THE COOK HIS ORDERS

牛肉割一斤、羊肉半斤、猪肉十二两

120 You may buy a catty of beef, half a catty of mutton, and twelve ounces of pork.

NIU² RU² GO² I² GIN¹, YANG² RU² BAN⁴ GIN¹, DJU¹ RU² SHǏ² ER⁴ LIANG³.

牛肉

NIU² RU²　　*lit.*, cow meat, and so on through the list. The word 肉 RU², is constantly corrupted in many parts of West China to ROU⁴, with the change to fourth tone. But the pronunciation RU² is understood. In Chinese we have no 'quarter of a catty' or 'three-quarters of a catty'; we must use the number of ounces.

還要稱猪油三斤

121 You are also to buy three catties of lard.

HAI² YAO⁴ CHEN¹ DJU¹ YIU² SAN¹ GIN¹.

Note the idiom by which the name of the object comes first after the verb, followed by the quantity.

拿回來就熬出來

122 Bring it home and try it out.

LA² HWEI² LAI² DZIU¹ NGAO² CHU² LAI².

熬

NGAO²　　ordinarily in this tone, but constantly spoken in the first tone.

现在，市上有晾子水果

123　What fruit is there in the market now?

　　HSIEN⁴ DZAI⁴, SHĬ⁴ SHANG⁴ YIU³ SHA⁴ DZ³ SHUI³ GO³?

现 在

HSIEN⁴ DZAI⁴　about the most used term for 'now'; 如今 RU² GIN¹, is also much used, and is usually supposed to refer to longer periods of time,—as *now* in relation to last year, or *now* in relation to last century, etc.

市 上

SHĬ⁴ SHANG⁴　market on, in the market.

水 果

SHUI³ GO³　*lit.*, water fruit, as distinguished from. 乾果 GAN¹ GO³ dry fruit, that is nuts.

现在水果不多，只有橘子橙柑

124　Just now there is not much fruit; there are only oranges, (two kinds).

　　HSIEN⁴ DZAI⁴ SHUI³ GO³ BU² DO¹; GĬ³ YIU³ GŪ² DZ³, TSEN² GAN¹.

GIVING THE COOK HIS ORDERS

只

GĬ³   only; always used at the beginning of a sentence. Other common words having this meaning are 光 GWANG¹, 單 DAN¹, 不過 BU² GO⁴.

後來有啥子

125 What (fruit) will there be after a while?
HOU⁴ LAI² YIU³ SHA⁴ DZ³?

後來

HOU⁴ LAI²   afterwards. Other common words are 以後 I³ HOU⁴, 過後 GO⁴ HOU⁴, 隨後 SUI² HOU⁴, all much used.

後來有櫻桃、枇杷、杏子、桃子、花紅、萍果、葡萄、柿子、李子、毛李子、梨子、石榴、氣柑

126 After a while there will be cherries, loquats, apricots, peaches, apples, sweet apples, grapes, persimmons, plums, "hairy plums", pears, pomegranates, and pumelos.

HOU⁴ LAI² YIU³ YIN¹ TAO², PI² BA¹, HEN⁴ DZ³, TAO² DZ³, HWA¹ HUNG², PIN² GO³, PU² TAO², SHĬ⁴ DZ³, LI³ DZ³, MAO² LI³ DZ³, LI² DZ³, SHĬ⁴ LIU², CHI⁴ GAN¹.

    This is merely a list of some of the most common fruits, without any attempt to be exhaustive.

櫻 桃

YIN¹ TAO²   constantly corrupted to NGEN¹ TAO² or NGEN¹ TER². 梨子 LI² DZ³, pears, also constantly called LI² ER², possibly to distinguish readily from the term for plums. 葡萄 PU² TAO², grapes,—the second character is most often put into the first tone, for euphony's sake.

菜有那幾樣

127   What vegetables are there (just now)?

TSAI⁴ YIU³ LA³ GI² YANG⁴?

菜

TSAI¹   the common word for vegetables of all sorts.

     Note the third tone of 那 LA³, here, because it is interrogative.

我們四川的菜多

128   We have a great many different kinds of vegetables in Szechwan.

NGO³ MEN² SI¹ CHWAN¹ DY² TSAI⁴ DO¹.

     Lit., Our "Szechwan vegetables are numerous". The little possessive particle 的 DY², is understood after 我們 NGO³ MEN². The meaning is really that the *kinds* of vegetables are numerous.

GIVING THE COOK HIS ORDERS

有洋芋、紅苕、豌豆、黃豆、玉麥、(包穀)紅蘿蔔、白蘿蔔、葱子、芹菜、青菜、白菜、蓮花白、黃瓜、東瓜、南瓜、茄子、撇南

129 There are potatoes, sweet potatoes, peas, yellow beans, corn, carrots, turnips, onions, celery, green vegetable, Chinese cabbage, cabbage, cucumbers, winter squash, squash, egg-plant, kohl rabi.

This also is a very short list of some of the commonest vegetables, of which there is such an abundant variety in Szechwan.

玉麥
YŬ[4] ME[2]　　corn, so called at and about Chengtu only; elsewhere the term 包穀 BAO[1] GU[2], generally prevails.

YIU[3] YANG[2] YŬ[4], HUNG[2] SHAO[2], WAN[1] DOU[4], HWANG[2] DOU[4], YŬ[4] ME[2], (BAO[1] GU[2]), HUNG[2] LO[2] BU[4], BE[2] LO[2] BU[4], TSUNG[1] DZ[3], TSIN[2] TSAI[4], TSIN[1] TSAI[4], BE[2] TSAI[4], LIEN[2] HWA[1] BE[2], HWANG[2] GWA[1], DUNG[1] GWA[1], LAN[2] GWA[1], CHIE[2] DZ[3], PIE[3] LAN[2].

王長興、可以買一本賬簿子、記賬

130 Wang Chang-Hsin, you may buy an account-book (in which) to keep your accounts.

WANG[2] CHANG[2] HSIN[1], KO[3] I[3] MAI[3] I[2] BEN[3] DJANG[4] BU[4] DZ[3] GI[4] DJANG[4].

賬
DJANG⁴　　　account. 賬簿子 DJANG⁴ BU⁴ DZ³, account book.

記
GI⁴　　　to record, to remember.

本
BEN³　　　classifier for book.

天天晚上要算賬

131　We shall reckon accounts every evening.
TIEN¹ TIEN¹ WAN³ SHANG⁴ YAO⁴ SWAN⁴ DJANG⁴.

天天
TIEN¹ TIEN¹　　day day, *i.e.* daily.

晚上
WAN³ SHANG⁴　　evening on, *i.e.* in the evening.

算
SWAN⁴　　　to reckon, to calculate.

Some people take accounts once a week, others once a month only. Others again who are fond of accuracy in keeping accounts prefer to reckon daily.

還有一句要緊的話

132　I have another important thing to say to you.
HAI² YIU³ I² GÜ⁴ YAO⁴ GIN³ DY² HWA⁴.

Lit., Still there is one sentence important words.

GIVING THE COOK HIS ORDERS

句
GÜ⁴   classifier for sentence or phrase.

要緊
YAO⁴ GIN³   important. Very common, as is also the negative, 不要緊 BU² YAO⁴ GIN³, it is of no importance. A very similar phrase is 沒來頭 MU² LAI² TOU², it does not matter.

你花好多錢,要報好多錢

133 You are to report exactly the amounts you spend.

NI³ HWA¹ HAO³ DO¹ TSIEN², YAO⁴ BAO⁴ HAO³ DO¹ TSIEN².

Lit., You spend how much money, want report how much money.

花
HWA¹   to spend; flowers. 花錢 HWA¹ TSIEN², to spend money,—very common,—both phrase and act, in China.

報
BAO⁴   to report; a newspaper or magazine.

萬不可吃雷

134 You must not under any circumstances make a "squeeze".

Lit., Ten thousand not can eat thunder.

WAN⁴ BU² KO³ CHÏ² LUI².

萬
WAN⁴ an emphatic particle,—in constant use.

不可
BU² KO³ you may not, you must not.

吃雷
CHĪ² LUI² *lit.*, to eat thunder,—one of the commonest phrases meaning to make a profit out of funds that do not belong to one.

你願意人怎樣待你，
你也要怎樣待人

135 Whatsoever ye would that men should do unto you, even so do ye also unto them.

NI³ YUEN⁴ I⁴ REN² DZEN³ YANG⁴ DAI⁴ NI³, NI³ YE³ YAO⁴ DZEN³ YANG⁴ DAI⁴ REN².

LESSON 6. 第 六 課

掃 地
Sweeping the Floor

掃地

130 Sweeping the floor.

SAO³ DI⁴.

地

DI⁴   ground, but constantly used in this connection for floor, probably because most Chinese floors are just the earth, board floors being limited to the homes of the rich.

趙興順,拿掃把來

137 Djao Hsin-Shwen, bring the broom.

DJAO⁴ HSIN¹ SHWEN⁴ LA² SAO⁴ BA³ LAI².

掃把

SAO⁴ BA³   broom. Note that the same character is read SAO⁴, fourth tone, as the noun, broom, and SAO³, third tone as the verb 'to sweep.'

075

每天青早，要掃這個地

138 You are to sweep this floor every morning.
MEI³ TIEN¹ TSIN¹ DZAO³ YAO⁴ SAO³ DJE⁴ GO⁴ DI⁴.

每天
MEI³ TIEN¹   each day, every day. Also 天天 TIEN¹ TIEN¹, same meaning, very common.

青早
TSIN¹ DZAO³   bright and early; 早 DZAO³, early.

要
YAO⁴   want; I want you to; you are required; etc.

東西要蹧開掃

139 You must move things out of the way when you sweep.
DUNG¹ SI¹ YAO⁴ DZAN³ KAI¹ SAO³.

東西
DUNG¹ SI¹   lit., east west, things, articles.

蹧開
DZAN³ KAI¹   lit., move open, i.e. move away from their original place. The genius of the language seems to require a final 掃 SAO³, in order to round off the sense.

SWEEPING THE FLOOR

椅子耍趱開掃

140 You must move the chairs while you sweep.

I³ DZ³ YAO⁴ DZAN³ KAI¹ SAO³.

Exactly the same construction as the last sentence, but specifying chairs. Note that the important word in the sentence, 椅子 chairs, ~~chairs~~, comes first, and what is to be said about them afterwards.

茶機抬開掃

141 You must move the tea-tables when sweeping.

CHA² GI¹ TAI² KAI¹ SAO³.

茶機

CHA² GI¹   lit., tea bench; the little square tables always placed between two chairs in a Chinese guest room.

抬開

TAI² KAI¹   lift aside. Not "move aside" as before but lift aside. Same construction as before, only that the 耍 is omitted.

角角上耍掃乾乾淨淨的

142 You should sweep the corners very clean.

GO² GO² SHANG⁴ YAO⁴ SAO³ GAN¹ GAN¹ DZIN⁴ DZIN⁴ DY².

角

GO²   a horn of a cow or sheep; here a corner. The word is constantly duplicated in this way in speech. The 上 SHANG³, is the 'on' or 'in' the corner.

CHINESE LESSONS

乾淨
GAN¹ DZIN⁴   clean, the commonest every-day word having this meaning; here duplicated for emphasis. Very common.

掃歸一了,就把東西還原

143 When you have finished sweeping put things back where they belong.

SAO³ GWEI¹ I² LIAO³ DZIU⁴ BA³ DUNG¹ SI¹ HWAN² YUEN².

歸一
GWEI¹ I²   finished, completed, all in order. Very common.

還
HWAN²   to replace, restore.

原
YUEN²   origin or original.

跟倒就搣灰

144 Then proceed to dust immediately after.
GEN¹ DAO³ DZIU⁴ MA² HWEI¹.

跟倒
GEN¹ DAO³   lit., to follow after; hence the use here,—'Follow right after' with your dusting. This little phrase is in very common use in just this meaning,—say 'immediately', or 'at once'.

SWEEPING THE FLOOR

撒灰

MA² HWEI¹　　wipe dust, i.e. dust,—the verb.

掃的時候,要把掃把撐倒掃

145　When sweeping, you should press down on the broom.

SAO³ DY² SHĪ² HOU⁴, YAO⁴ BA³ SAO⁴ BA³ TSEN³ DAO³ SAO³.

　　Note the relative 'when', 的時候 DY² SHĪ² HOU⁴. This phrase never begins a sentence.

撐

TSEN³　　to press down. 倒 DAO³, makes it into a dissyllable, and also shows completed action. This character is adapted to this meaning; that is to say, this word TSEN³, has no proper character, although it is a common word in conversation.

不要把灰挑起來

146　Do not cause the dust to fly up.

BU² YAO⁴ BA³ HWEI¹ TIAO¹ CHI³ LAI².

挑

TIAO¹　　properly to carry on the shoulder by means of a pole; but adapted or borrowed here to express this meaning.

起來

CHI³ LAI²　　to rise, to get up,—in the morning for instance. Here applied to the rising of the dust in the air.

灰塵不要撲起來,纔好

147 The dust should not rise up in a cloud.
HWEI¹ CHEN² BU² YAO⁴ PU² CHI³ LAI² TSAI² HAO³.

灰 塵

HWEI¹ CHEN²   the full word for dust, constantly cut short by the use of the one word 灰 HWEI¹.

撲 起 來

PU² CHI³ LAI²   to rise in a cloud, as dust and therefore slightly different from 挑 起 來 TIAO¹ CHI³ LAI², to flirt or beat up into the air.

纔

TSAI²   then and not till then; a most useful little word, and comprehensive. It may often be translated by the single word 'then', as here: 纔 好 TSAI² HAO³, then good, then it will be satisfactory.

把灰塵掃成一堆

148 Sweep the dust into a heap.
BA³ HWEI¹ CHEN² SAO³ CHEN² I² DUI¹.

掃 成

SAO³ CHEN²   sweep into; *lit.*, sweep become.

一 堆

I² DUI¹   a pile, a heap.

SWEEPING THE FLOOR

拿撮箕來

149 Bring the dust pan.

LA² TSO² GI¹ LAI².

撮箕

TSO² GI¹   dust pan, whether made of tin or of woven bamboo.

把灰撮起來

150 Take the dust up in the dust-pan.

BA³ HWEI¹ TSO² CHI³ LAI².

撮

TSO²   to scoop up as by a scoop or dust-pan. Hence 撮箕 TSO² GI¹, scoop basket, dust-pan. The Chinese dust-pan is properly made of woven bamboo.

端到外頭去倒

151 Carry it outside and empty it.

DWAN¹ DAO⁴ WAI⁴ TOU² CHŬ⁴ DAO⁴.

端

DWAN¹   to carry with the arms extended in front, as a package, a lamp, or, as in this case, a dust-pan.

外頭

WAI⁴ TOU²   outside; 裏頭 LI³ TOU², inside; 前頭 TSIEN² TOU², in front; 後頭 HOU⁴ TOU², behind. Each one of these is very commonly preceded by 在 DZAI⁴, in, at, on; 在外頭 DZAI⁴ WAI⁴ TOU², on the outside; 在裏頭 DZAI⁴ LI³ TOU², on the inside; etc. Here we have 到外頭 DAO⁴ WAI⁴ TOU², to the outside.

倒

DAO⁴ to empty.

把掃把,撮箕,撿好

152 Put the broom and dust-pan carefully away.
BA³ SAO⁴ BA³, TSO² GI¹, GIEN³ HAO³.

撿

GIEN³ to put away, to pick up, to select; a very common word in some one or all of these senses.

撿好

GIEN³ HAO³ perhaps a little more accurately translated, 'put away properly'. A variation is 好生撿 HAO³ SEN¹ GIEN³, lit.. carefully put away, a most excellent little phrase much needed by the missionary who has a servant in training. It may be used in regard to any article whatsoever.

Note the absence of any word representing 'and' between broom and dust pan in this sentence. Chinese idiom does not require it; but the use of the little word 給 GE¹, 'and' is quite allowable and much used in just this situation.

LESSON 7. 第七課

洗地
Washing the Floor

洗地

153 Washing the floor.

SI^3 DI^4.

洗

SI^3 to wash, and 地 DI^4, the ground, the earth, the floor.

要洗地

YAO^4 SI^3 DI^4 I want you to wash the floor, you are to wash the floor, or I am about to wash the floor. All are equally good translations. It all depends on who the speaker is, and what are the circumstances connected with its use.

趙興順, 過來一下

154 Djao Hsin-Shwen, come over here.

DJAO^4 HSIN^1 SHWEN^4, GO^4 LAI^2 I^2 HA^4.

過

GO⁴ to pass over; 來 LAI², come; 過來 GO⁴ LAI², come over here—a very mild way of calling your coolie or cook to you. The command is still further toned down by the addition of the 一下 I² HA⁴, a little, *i.e.* for a moment. The Chinese official says 來 LAI²; the business man 過來 GO⁴ LAI²; and the kind-hearted employer 過來一下 GO⁴ LAI² I² HA⁴. There is no question as to which form the missionary should use.

這個地陣, 每天要洗一回

155 I want you to wash this floor daily.

DJE⁴ GO⁴ DI⁴ DJEN⁴ MEI³ TIEN¹ YAO⁴ SI³ I² HWEI².

地陣

DI⁴ DJEN⁴ the dissyllable for floor, conveniently used when one is speaking of more than one floor. It is more *particular* in its meaning than the single word 地 DI⁴, which is very general.

一回

I² HWEI² one time, once; very common. *Lit.*, each day want wash one time.

提一桶乾淨水來

156 Bring a pail of clean water.

TI² I² TUNG³ GAN¹ DZIN⁴ SHUI³ LAI².

WASHING THE FLOOR

提
TI²   to carry; used of any article which has a handle or bail, as a pitcher or a pail, and which is carried with the arm hanging straight down. If the pitcher is small and is carried with hand extended in front of one, as one carries a lamp, then we use 端 DWAN¹, (See No. 151). As a matter of fact, the article carried does not need to possess a handle; a sedan chair is carried sometimes when empty by the men with arms hanging straight down, 提 TI².

一 桶
I² TUNG³   a pail, one pail. Literally, 'Carry a pail clean water come.'

用 這 個 布 作 洗 地 帕 子

157   You may use this cloth as a floor cloth.
YUNG⁴ DJE⁴ GO⁴ BU⁴ DZO² SI³ DI⁴ PA⁴ DZ³.

用
YUNG⁴   use, to use; very common.

這 個 布
DJE⁴ GO⁴ BU²   lit., this cotton cloth, i.e. this piece of cloth. 作 DZO², as, to act as; 帕子 PA⁴ DZ³, cloth, any kind of a towel, wash cloth, handkerchief, serviette, etc. Here it is 洗地帕子 SI³ DI⁴ PA⁴ DZ³, wash floor cloth. 洗臉帕 SI³ LIEN³ PA⁴, face cloth, which every Chinese carries. 乾帕子 GAN¹ PA⁴ DZ³, lit., dry cloth, i.e. towel. 手帕子 SHOU³ PA⁴ DZ³ handkerchief. 手巾 SHOU³ GIN¹, 'serviette, a name adopted by many to distinguish from 手帕子.

CHINESE LESSONS

拿布打濕水

158 Wet the floor cloth.
LA² BU⁴ DA³ SHÏ² SHUI³.
   Lit., 'Bring the cloth, strike wet water.'

拿
LA²   to carry, as any light article may be carried in the hand.

打濕
DA³ SHÏ²   to wet. It is curious that the word 水 SHUI³, water, should be used after the 打濕 DA³ SHÏ², to wet; because wetting rarely occurs with anything other than water. One can only say that it is not an absolute necessity, 水 SHUI³, may be omitted.

糾一下

159 Wring it a little.
GIU³ I² HA⁴.

糾
GIU³   to wring; ordinarily in first tone; and its use in this sense of to wring, is rather strained. But this is a common *word*, spoken always in the third tone, whether this is the proper character, or whether there is any character.

拿來把地陣板認眞洗乾淨

160 Bring it (the cloth) and honestly wash the floor boards clean.
LA² LAI² BA³ DI⁴ DJEN⁴ BAN³ REN⁴ DJEN¹ SI³ GAN¹ DZIN⁴.

WASHING THE FLOOR.

拿來
LA² LAI²   bring; here rather in the nature of an introduction.

地陣板
DI⁴ DJEN⁴ BAN³ floor boards. 認真 REN⁴ DJEN¹, *lit.*, to be in earnest, to be faithful, faithfully, honestly. A common phrase.

洗一下地陣、又要把帕子洗乾淨

161 After washing the floor for a little, you must wash the cloth clean.

SI³ I² HA⁴ DI⁴ DJEN⁴, YIU⁴ YAO⁴ BA³ PA⁴ DZ³ SI³ GAN¹ DZIN⁴.

又
YIU⁴   also, again; perhaps the most common word having this meaning. Note the non-expression of the word 'after' at the beginning; or if it were expressed in Chinese, it would most likely come after the first phrase, as 以後 I³ HOU⁴, or 過後 GO⁴ HOU⁴, However, Chinese spoken language most frequently leaves such words as 'after', 'if' 'when' understood, not expressed. Chinese is nothing if not brief, condensed.

水髒了的時候、提出去換

162 When the water is dirty, carry it out and get clean water. (*Lit.*, 'exchange' for clean water).

SHUI³ DZANG¹ LIAO³ DY² SHĪ² HOU⁴, TI² CHU² CHÜ⁴ HWAN⁴.

髒

DZANG[1] dirty, about the most common word for this meaning. Note the 的時候 DY[2] SHĬ[2] HOU[4], relative 'when', always at the end of the phrase, not at the beginning as in English. 提出去 TI[2] CHU[2] CHŬ[4], to carry out; *lit.*, carry go out go; surely clear enough and strong enough. 換 HWAN[4], to exchange, to change, very common.

洗地的時候,要把東西趲開洗

163 When you wash the floor you should move things aside in order to wash (thoroughly).

SI[3] DI[4] DY[2] SHĬ[2] HOU[4], YAO[4] BA[3] DUNG[1] SI[1] DZAN[3] KAI[1] SI[3].

See No. 139 for this construction. The words 'in order to' are understood before the last character 洗 SI[3]. 要 YAO[4], here translated 'you should'.

洗過了,就要還原

164 After you have washed (the floor) you must put things back (where they belong).

SI[3] GO[4] LIAO[3], DZIU[4] YAO[4] HWAN[2] YUEN[2].

就

DZIU[1] then, immediately, not translated here. 要 YAO[4], here translated 'you must'. 還 HWAN[2], replace; 原 YUEN[2], original; from which the meaning of the combination is easily deduced.

WASHING THE FLOOR

角角上要好生洗乾淨

165 You must be careful to wash the corners clean.

GO² GO² SHANG⁴ YAO¹ HAO³ SEN¹ SI³ GAN¹ DZIN⁴.

See No. 142. 好生 HAO³ SEN¹, be careful, carefully; perhaps the most common word for 'be careful' in use about the house. 把細 BA³ SI⁴, be careful, take care; also very common. 小心 SIAO³ SIN¹, be careful; 細心 SI⁴ SIN¹, be careful. The last two are used, but not so frequently. Note that the word 好生 HAO³ SEN¹, comes before the verb.

洗的時候,棹子脚脚不打髒

166 When you are washing (the floor), you must not dirty the legs of the table.

SI³ DY² SHI² HOU⁴, DJO² DZ³ GIO² GIO¹ BU² YAO⁴ DA³ DZANG¹.

棹子

DJO² DZ³ table. 脚 foot, whether of a person or of a table or chair. It is very commonly duplicated in this way, when used of a thing; and single, usually, when used of a person. 打髒 DA³ DZANG¹, to dirty; 打髒了的 DA³ DZANG¹ LIAO³ DY², it is dirty or dirtied.

水不要用多了

167 Do not use too much water.

SHUI³ BU² YAO⁴ YUNG⁴ DO¹ LIAO³.

Note that the sentence begins with the most important word, 水 SHUI³, the thing being talked about. 用 YUNG⁴, to use; 多 DO¹, much; 多了 DO¹ LIAO³ too much. The other common expression for 'too much' is 太多 TAI⁴ DO¹. Or even 太多了 TAI⁴ DO¹ LIAO³. But the first is most used, simply 多了 DO¹ LIAO³.

隨洗隨搣乾

168 Wipe it dry as you wash.
SUI² SI³ SUI² MA² GAN¹.

隨

SUI²　　　　　to follow; in book and pulpit language often combined with 跟 GEN¹, as 跟 隨 GEN¹ SUI², the dissyllable meaning to follow. Here the two characters 隨 SUI²..隨 SUI², may be translated, as ... so, as you wash, so wipe; *i.e.* wipe as you wash. 搣乾 MA² GAN¹, wipe dry.

地乾了，總要看不倒花的，纔好

169 When the floor is dry, one should not be able to see any streaks.
DI⁴ GAN¹ LIAO³, DZUNG³ YAO⁴ KAN⁴ BU² DAO³ HWA¹ DY² TSAI² HAO³.

The three character phrase, 的時候 DY² SHI² HOU⁴, when, is understood after the character 了 LIAO³. 總 DZUNG³, an emphatic particle.

看不倒

KAN⁴ BU² DAO³, cannot see, 花的 HWA¹ DY², *lit.*, 'flowered', here 'streaked' or streaks.

This little character 的 DY², although in the second tone, is constantly spoken in the first tone, as here, for euphony.

WASHING THE FLOOR

纔好

TSAI² HAO³   then that will be satisfactory.

情願慢點,把地洗得乾乾淨淨的

170 I prefer that you work a little more slowly, and wash the floor very clean.

TSIN² YUEN⁴ MAN⁴ DIEN³ BA³ DI⁴ SI³ DE² GAN¹ GAN¹ DZIN⁴ DZIN⁴ DY².

情願

TSIN² YUEN⁴   I prefer, we prefer, to prefer; very common.

慢點

MAN⁴ DIEN³   more slowly; *lit.,* slow a little. Note the emphasis on the word 'clean' by duplicating the characters.

厨房,餐房,書房,睡房,這幾個地陣

171 The kitchen, dining room, study and bed room,—all these floors

CHU² FANG², TSAN¹ FANG², SHU¹ FANG², SHUI⁴ FANG², DJE⁴ GI³ GO⁴ DI⁴ DJEN⁴

這幾個地陣

DJE⁴ GI³ GO⁴ DI⁴ DJEN⁴   these several floors. This is only part of the sentence, being continued as No. 172. It is therefore awkward to translate.

CHINESE LESSONS

天天都要洗

172 should be washed every day.

TIEN¹ TIEN¹ DU¹ YAO⁴ SI³.

This is the completion of No. 171. 都 DU¹, all; one of the many terms for 'all' in Chinese. One would suppose that it would be quite sufficient to say 天天 TIEN¹ TIEN¹, daily. But the Chinese seems to need an 'all' to properly emphasize the idea of 'daily'. This sort of construction occurs again and again, with words for 'all' and with other words.

客廳地陣,一個星期洗兩回

173 The floor of the parlor is to be washed twice a week.

KE² TIN¹ DI⁴ DJEN⁴ I² GO⁴ SIN¹ CHI¹ SI³ LIANG³ HWEI².

客廳
KE² TIN¹ parlor or sitting room. This is much better, than 客堂 KE² TANG², which smacks of a temple. 客廳 KE² TIN¹, or 花廳 HWA¹ TIN¹, is the term used by the better class Chinese for their guest rooms in their compounds or 公舘 GUNG¹ GWAN³.

星期
SIN¹ CHI¹ week, the new term which is superseding 禮拜 LI³ BAI⁴ in this sense. 禮拜 LI³ BAI⁴, has been used in at least three senses; it is a welcome relief to get a new term so happily chosen as 星期 SIN¹ CHI¹ which if not Christian is certainly not non-Christian, and may be unhesitatingly adopted.

把幾個地陣洗歸一了

174 When you have finished washing the several floors

BA³ GI³ GO⁴ DI⁴ DJEN⁴ SI³ GWEI¹ I² LIAO³.

This sentence is not complete; it is continued and finished in No. 175. The phrase 的時侯 DY² SHÎ² HOU⁴ is understood at the end of this sentence, 'when', which in English is placed at the beginning. In English another word is properly understood, 'these' 這 DJE⁴, between 把 BA³ and 幾 GI³; it would then read, "When you have washed these several floors". Chinese idiom prefers to omit it.

就把帕子洗乾淨，晾起

175 Then wash the cloth clean and hang it out to dry.

DZIU⁴ BA³ PA⁴ DZ³ SI³ GAN¹ DZIN⁴ LANG⁴ CHI³.

It is curious that the word 乾淨 GAN¹ DZIN⁴, clean, seems to be required in Chinese after 洗 SI³, every time. I think this is an illustration of the constant tendency on the part of spoken Chinese to get away from the monosyllable. 洗 SI³, is too small and short a word to stand all by itself; hence the ever-recurring 洗乾淨 SI³ GAN¹ DZIN⁴. Why should we not say 洗帕子 SI³ PA⁴ DZ³? So we may, but not 洗帕子乾淨 SI³ PA⁴ DZ³ GAN¹ DZIN⁴; this construction is quite contrary to the genius of Chinese. We must break it in two with a 把 BA³, as above.

晾起

LANG⁴ CHI³   to hang up or out to dry, whether in or out of the sun; 晾起 LIANG⁴ CHI³, exactly the same; both much used; 曬起 SHAI⁴ CHI³ to hang out in the sun.

把水提去倒了

176 Carry the water out and empty it.
BA³ SHUI³ TI² CHŬ⁴ DAO⁴ LIAO³.

提

TI² to carry, with arms hanging down and the article suspended, as a pail. 倒 DAO⁴, to empty. 提去 TI¹ CHŬ⁴, carry go, *i.e.* carry out. Why the 了 LIAO³ after the 倒 DAO⁴? It is certainly not past tense here. I think about the best hint is that here again we see an evidence of the effort to get away from the monosyllable, to a polysyllabic form, or at least to a dissyllable.

把水桶掀好

177 Put the water pail away properly.
BA³ SHUI³ TUNG³ GIEN³ HAO³.

Compare No. 152 and No. 164.

LESSON 8. 第八課

撮灰
Dusting

撮灰

178 Dusting.

MA² HWEI¹.

撮

MA²   to wipe, constantly used in speech, but rarely met with, if at all, in the written language. 灰 HWEI¹, dust; the complete two character word is 灰塵 HWEI¹ CHEN², which is used freely, as well as the single character.

要先掃地、後纔拿水來洗

179 You are required to sweep first, then bring water and wash (the floor);

YAO⁴ SIEN¹ SAO³ DI⁴, HOU⁴ TSAI² LA² SHUI³ LAI² SI³.

先

SIEN¹   first, a most useful little word, much needed by beginners.

後

HOU⁴ after, afterwards; the two character word is very common, 以後 I³ HOU⁴, or 過後 GO⁴ HOU⁴. Compare No. 161. 纔 TSAI², then, or in full, 'then and not till then'.

在後, 搣灰

180 and finally to dust.

DZAI⁴ HOU⁴ MA² HWEI¹

在後

DZAI⁴ HOU⁴ at afterwards, *i.e.* finally.

拿搣灰帕子來

181 Bring the dust cloth.

LA² MA² HWEI¹ PA⁴ DZ³ LAI².

It is not sufficient to say 灰帕子 HWEI¹ PA⁴ DZ³, *lit.*, dust cloth, as we do in English; we must say 搣灰帕子 MA² HWEI¹ PA⁴ DZ³, wipe dust cloth. 拿來 LA² LAI², to bring, used for any light article; 提來 TI² LAI², to bring, as a pail; 抬來 TAI² LAI², to bring, as a heavier article, as a chair, a bench. Note how the two parts of this verb are separated, and the name of the article inserted between.

棹子上的灰, 要搣乾淨

182 You are to dust the table clean.

DJO² DZ³ SHANG⁴ DY² HWEI¹ YAO⁴ MA² GAN¹ DZIN⁴.

Lit., The on-table's dust, want wipe clean.

The full phrase for 'on the table' is 在棹子上 DZAI⁴ DJO² DZ³ SHANG⁴, here cut short by the omission of 在 DZAI⁴.

DUSTING

棹子上的東西、挨一挨二的拿起來、纔撮灰

183 In order to dust properly, you should take the articles up one by one from the table.

DJO² DZ³ SHANG⁴ DY² DUNG¹ SI¹, NGAI¹ I² NGAI¹ ER⁴ DY² LA² CHI³ LAI², TSAI² MA² HWEI¹.

Lit., The on-table things, in regular order take up, then dust. 挨一挨二的 NGAI¹ I² NGAI¹ ER⁴ DY², in regular order, one after another. 拿起來 LA² CHI³ LAI², to take up; 拿來 LA² LAI², to bring; 拿倒 LA² DAO³, to take hold of.

撮灰的時候、樣樣東西都要拿起來、或是趲開

184 When dusting, everything must be taken up or moved to one side.

MA² HWEI¹ DY² SHÍ² HOU⁴, YANG⁴ YANG⁴ DUNG¹ SI¹ DU¹ YAO⁴ LA² CHI³ LAI², HWE² SHÍ⁴ DZAN³ KAI¹.

樣樣
YANG⁴ YANG⁴   each kind, every kind or sort.
Lit: sort, sort. Note the use of 都 DU¹, again, after 'everything'. Compare No. 172.

趲開
DZAN³ KAI¹, move aside; very common.

棹子脚脚、要撮乾淨

185 You must dust the table legs clean. (Compare No. 166).

DJO² DZ³ GIO² GIO¹ YAO¹ MA² GAN¹ DZIN⁴.

脚

GIO² is ordinarily in the second tone; but as often happens in these duplicated characters, the second one falls into a different tone for euphony's sake; it would be hard to say 脚脚 GIO² GIO², both in the low tone; but it becomes easy when the second one goes up into the first tone.

椅子耍搣乾淨

186 The chairs are to be dusted clean.

I³ DZ³ YAO⁴ MA² GAN¹ DZIN⁴.

椅子的脚脚、横横、靠背、各處縫縫、都耍搣乾淨

187 The legs, cross-pieces and backs of the chairs, together with all the crevices, must be dusted clean.

I³ DZ³ DY² GIO² GIO¹ KWAN⁴ KWAN¹, KAO⁴ BEI⁴, GO² CHU⁴ FUNG⁴ FUNG¹, DU¹ YAO⁴ MA² GAN¹ DZIN⁴.

横横

KWAN⁴ KWAN¹ cross-pieces. The tones are marked as spoken. This character is adapted, being ordinarily read HWANG² or HWANG⁴, or HWAN². 靠背 KAO⁴ BEI⁴, the lean-back, *i.e.* the back. 各處縫縫 GO² CHU⁴ FUNG⁴ FUNG¹, *lit.*, every place crevice. Again the tone of the second FUNG⁴ is marked as spoken,—for euphony's sake.

DUSTING

書架子、櫃子、撴乾淨

188 The book case and the cabinet are to be dusted clean.

SHU¹ GIA⁴ DZ³, GWEI⁴ DZ³, MA² GAN¹ DZIN⁴.

書架子

SHU¹ GIA⁴ DZ³ book case ; *lit.,* 'book frame-work'. 櫃子 GWEI⁴ DZ³, any kind of a cupboard, cabinet, dresser, sideboard, etc.

爐子高頭的臺臺、也要撴乾淨

189 The mantel above the grate is also to be dusted clean.

LU² DZ³ GAO¹ TOU² DY² TAI² TAI¹, YE³ YAO⁴ MA² GAN¹ DZIN⁴.

爐子

LU² DZ³ stove, grate; 高頭 GAO¹ TOU², above; 臺臺 TAI² TAI¹, ledge, platform. *Lit,* 'The above-stove-ledge'. 也 YE³, also; very similar to 又 YIU⁴ ; but the sense of 'again' is rather prominent in 又 YIU⁴ ; it is not in 也 YE³. Note change to first tone of the second 臺 TAI², for euphony.

臺臺上擱的東西、要拿開撴灰

190 The articles placed on the mantel must be moved in order to dust.

TAI² TAI¹ SHANG⁴ KO⁴ DY² DUNG¹ SI¹, YAO⁴ LA² KAI¹ MA² HWEI¹.

拿 開

LA² KAI¹ to take away, to remove; thus differing slightly from the expression 趲 開 DZAN³ KAI¹; the latter indicates rather a moving to one side, just shoved over, perhaps. Compare Nos. 163, 183, 184.

撳灰帕子,要不要的拿倒外頭去,抖乾淨

191 Take your dust cloth outside occasionally and shake it clean.

MA² HWEI¹ PA⁴ DZ,³ YAO⁴ BU² YAO⁴ DY² LA² DAO³ WAI⁴ TOU² CHÜ⁴, TOU³ GAN¹ DZIN⁴.

撳 灰 帕 子

MA² HWEI¹ PA⁴ DZ³ may be shortened to 撳灰帕 MA² HWEI¹ PA⁴, if you prefer. 要不要的 YAO⁴ BU² YAO⁴ DY², occasionally, every now and then, a very common phrase and very useful.

間 或

GIEN⁴ HWEI² has exactly the same meaning, and is a trifle more polished. I have marked the 的 DY², in second tone, as usual; but as a matter of fact it is very apt to rise to first tone for euphony's sake.

灰撳歸一了,把帕子掛起

192 When you have finished dusting, hang up your dust cloth.

HWEI¹ MA² GWEI¹ I² LIAO³, BA³ PA⁴ DZ³ GWA⁴ CHI³.

DUSTING

Note the beginning of the sentence with the noun 灰 HWEI[1], which tells us at once the subject of the remark. 'When' is, as before, the translation of 的時侯 DY[2] SHI[2] HOU[4], understood after 了 LIAO[3].

掛起
GWA[4] CHI[3]　　to hang up, as a cloth, a garment, etc.

撣灰,萬不可用担帚子

193　When dusting, you must not on any account use a feather duster.

MA[2] HWEI[1], WAN[4] BU[2] KO[3] YUNG[4] DAN[3] DJOU[1] DZ[3].

Again the relative 'when' 的時侯 DY[2] SHI[2] HOU[4], is understood after 撣灰 MA[2] HWEI[1]. 萬 WAN[4], *lit.*, ten thousand; here an emphatic particle. 不可用 BU[2] KO[3] YUNG[4], (you) may not use. 担帚子 DAN[3] DJOU[1] DZ[3], feather duster. Better give your new servant this warning, else he will likely make use of this very objectionable article all on his own account. Apart from its insanitary qualities, well known to us all, the feather duster in China is almost always made and sold by the poorest of the poor,—people who live amidst filth and disease.

囘囘要用帕子撣灰

194　You are always to use a cloth to dust.

HWEI[2] HWEI[2] YAO[4] YUNG[4] PA[4] DZ[3] MA[2] HWEI[1].

囘囘
HWEI[2] HWEI[2]　　every time, always.

要搣、不要挋

195　You should wipe, not flick the dust.

Yao⁴ Ma², Bu² Yao⁴ Chan³.

　　The emphasis is on the two verbs of course. The word for 'dust' is understood. 挋 CHAN³, to flick, to beat or strike. This character is not much used, but the word is very common. It is used also in the sentence 'Beat an egg', 挋蛋 CHAN³ DAN⁴.

先把氊子幾床、拿倒外頭去抖乾淨、隨後纔洗地陣

196　You should first take the rugs all outside and shake them clean, before washing the floor.

Sien¹ Ba³ Djan¹ Dz³ Gi³ Chwang², La² Dao³ Wai⁴ Tou² Chü⁴ Tou³ Gan¹ Dzin⁴, Sui² Hou⁴ Tsai² Si³ Di⁴ Djen⁴.

氊子

DJAN¹ DZ³　　rugs; sometimes called 地氊 DI⁴ DJAN¹, Lit., 'First take rugs several sheets, etc.' 床 CHWANG², bed, sheet, etc., here the classifier for rug. 抖 TOU³, to shake, as a rug or a table-cloth; to tremble.

氊子又要抖、又要晒

197　The rugs are to be both shaken and sunned.

Djan¹ Dz³ Yiu⁴ Yao⁴ Tou³, Yiu⁴ Yao⁴ Shai⁴.

DUSTING

叉
YIU⁴　　　叉 YIU⁴, both .... and ; very common. 晒 SHAI¹, to sun, to hang in the sun ; a very handy word, but this is no good reason why it should be incorporated into one's English vocabulary, even to the inclusion of 'shai-ed' and 'shai-ing'.

過後拿轉來還原

198 Afterwards bring them in and replace them.
GO⁴ HOU⁴ LA² DJWAN³ LAI² HWAN² YUEN².

過後
GO⁴ HOU⁴　　　afterwards. See No. 179. 拿轉來 LA² DJWAN³ LAI², bring back.

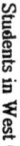

LESSON 9. 第九課

安置家具
Arranging the Furniture

安置家具

199 Arranging the Furniture.
NGAN¹ GĬ⁴ GIA¹ GŬ¹

安置

NGAN¹ GĬ⁴ to place, to arrange, to settle. 家具 GIA¹ GŬ¹, furniture, tools. 具 GŬ⁴, is in the fourth tone, but in this phrase 家具 GIA¹ GŬ¹, is commonly spoken in the first.

把棹子抬進來

200 Carry the table in.
BA³ DJO² DZ³ TAI²₍₃₁₎ DZIN⁴ LAI².

抬

TAI² to carry; used almost wholly of things carried by two or more persons. 抬來 TAI² LAI², bring, when speaking of such large or heavy articles. 抬進來 TAI² DZIN⁴ LAI², *lit.*, carry enter come, *i.e.* carry in.

擱在這裡

201 Put it here.

ARRANGING THE FURNITURE

擱 KO⁴, to put, to place; 放 FANG⁴, has exactly the same meaning, and these two words are constantly used, for all kinds of articles. 'It' is understood.

擱穩當，沒有

202 Is it placed firmly?

穩當 WEN³ DANG⁴, firm or firmly, steady, stable, solid, etc. Very common. 沒有 MU² YIU³, indicates that the sentence is interrogative.

不多穩當

203 It is not very firm.

Lit., Not much firm. 不多 BU²DO¹, is constantly used in this sense of 'not very, not much'.

找個東西墊這個脚脚

204 Get something to put under this leg.

找 DJAO³, to seek, to look for, to get. 墊 DIEN⁴, to place under, to wedge, an exceedingly useful word. It also means a cushion, and the connection between the two meanings is obvious, cushions are to be *placed under* people. The under sheet on the bed is 墊的 DIEN⁴ DY², just as the upper one is the 蓋的 GAI⁴ DY², *i.e.* the covering sheet.

把棹子墊穩當了

205 The table is wedged firmly.

To translate this sentence, 'You are to wedge the table firmly' would be equally correct. One must just judge by the preceding remark as to which is meant.

把灶抬到厨房頭來

206 Carry the cook-stove into the kitchen.

灶 DZAO⁴, the Chinese range, built of brick or stone, and therefore this term is appropriately used for the foreign cook-stove. The ordinary foreign heater or the grate may be appropriately called 爐子 LU² DZ³.

厨房 CHU² FANG², kitchen, a little more polished term than 灶房 DZAO⁴ FANG², but either may be used. The word 裏 LI³, is omitted before 頭 TOU²; the whole phrase would be 到厨房裏頭來 DAO⁴ CHU² FANG² LI³ TOU² LAI².

放倒

207 Put it down.

放 FANG⁴, to put, to place; 倒 DAO³, here expresses completed action. Compare No. 201.

把脚脚逗起

208 Fit the legs into place.

脚脚 GIO² GIO¹, legs of a piece of furniture. Note change of tone of the second character. 逗 DOU⁴, to fit together, to put into place, as a tenon into its mortise. This character can hardly be so explained; it has been borrowed because its sound and tone are right for this word.

好生抬起, 放不得手

209 Hold it up carefully; you must not let go.

好生 HAO³ SEN¹, carefully; 抬起 TAI² CHI³, to lift up, to hold up; 放 FANG⁴, here 'to let go'. Lit., let go must not hands; i.e. must not let go hands.

ARRANGING THE FURNITURE

脚脚逗好了，把灶抬起，
趱攏壁頭

210 When the feet are in place, lift the stove and move it over against the wall.

逗好了 DOU[4] HAO[3] LIAO[3], fitted into place; 趱攏 DZAN[3] LUNG[3], move to or against. Lit., move arrive at. 壁頭 BI[4] TOU[1], partition, i.e. the Chinese partition made of bamboo wattle with mud and lime plastered on one or both sides. In English we are apt to call the side of the house 'wall', whether made of plastered wattle or of brick.

Note change of tone of 頭 TOU[1], to first, for euphony.

朝右手拉一下

211 Pull towards the right hand a little.

朝 CHAO[2], towards; very common. 向 SIANG[4] has the same meaning and is used almost as frequently. 右 YIU[4], right; 左 DZO[3], left. 拉 LA[1], to pull, to drag; 扯 CHE[3] has exactly the same meaning, and the two are about equally used. The latter also means to tear,—as to tear paper, to tear cloth.

朝後頭掀一下

212 Push towards the back a little.

後頭 HOU[4] TOU[2], back, behind; the whole phrase is 在後頭 DZAI[4] HOU[4] TOU[2]. 掀 SUEN[1], to push, using the hands; a very common term. 捎 HSIAO[1], to push, is equally common; this term, however, may include the use of hands, shoulders, body, etc., in the process. 推 TUI[1], to push, as a wheelbarrow, an oar, etc. Used in this sense only for the process of pushing a vehicle or a utensil. This word 推 TUI¹, is the one *wenli* word meaning to push. The first two are rarely if ever found in books. Compare 掀 SUEN¹, to push, and 拴 SHWAN¹, to tie a knot. The tones are the same, but the sounds, while very similar, are yet quite distinct. Do not confuse them.

好, 對了

213 Good; that's right.

This use of 好 HAO³, is very similar to the use of 'good' or 'very good' in English, meaning that it is satisfactory. 對 DUI⁴, right, correct.

就是這個樣子

214 This is exactly right.

Lit., 'Then is this way'; *i.e.* 'this is *the* sort or fashion' which I wanted.

這一下子, 把烟冲安起

215 Now put on the stove-pipe.

這一下子 DJE⁴ I² HA⁴ DZ³, now, now then, an introductory word or phrase to the sentence, having no particular significance, any more than these English equivalents. 烟冲 YEN¹ CHUNG¹, smoke-pipe or brick chimney, and used also for the common iron stove-pipe. The word 鉄 TIEH², may be prefixed to indicate the latter. 安起 NGAN¹ CHI³, to put into place. 逗起 DOU⁴ CHI³, is also to put in place, but carries more of the idea of making a more or less firm connection.

把蓋蓋擱好

216 Put the covers on properly.

ARRANGING THE FURNITURE

蓋蓋 GAI⁴ GAI¹, a cover, a lid, whether singular or plural; 蓋子 GAI⁴ DZ³, is about equally used. 擱好 KO⁴ HAO³, to place properly.

把火門掛起

217 Hang the stove door.

Lit., Take fire door hang up.

拿刷子來, 把灶刷乾淨

218 Bring the brush and brush the stove clean.

刷子 SHWA² DZ³, a brush, whether stove-brush, boot-brush, clothes-brush, etc. But a hair brush is a 筧子 MIN³ DZ³, and to brush the hair is to 筧頭髮 MIN³ TOU² FA². We would not 刷頭髮 SHWA² TOU² FA², unless we had got dust into it!

用灶墨, 把灶刷亮

219 Use stove blacking and brush the stove till it shines.

灶墨 DZAO⁴ ME², *lit.*, stove ink. 刷亮 SHWA² LIANG⁴, to brush (till it) shines.

這一下子, 灶弄歸一了

220 Now then we have finished with the cook stove.

弄 LUNG¹, properly in the fourth tone, but here used in the first; this is a very useful all-round character; it may be translated 'to prepare', as food; to put to rights, to fix (in the North American sense). 歸一 GWEI¹ I², finished, completed, made neat or tidy.

LESSON 10. 第 十 課

堆箱子
Piling Boxes

堆箱子

221 Piling boxes.

堆 DUI¹, to pile, a pile; used as noun or verb indifferently. 箱子 SIANG¹ DZ³, boxes, a box; 篋篋 HSIA² HSIA¹, a small box, the cover of which draws out at the end, *e.g.* a match-box, a cake-box; 盒子 HO² DZ³, a small box, the cover of which lifts off, *e.g.* a baking powder tin. It may be round or square.

把箱子抬過來

222 Carry the boxes over here.

抬過來 TAI² GO⁴ LAI², *lit.*, carry pass come therefore 'carry over here'.

大的,兩個人抬一口

223 Two men may carry each of the large boxes.

大的 DA⁴ DY², with 'boxes' understood, the large boxes, the large ones. 兩個人 LIANG³ GO⁴ REN², two men, two people; 個 GO⁴, is the most common classifier. If you don't know any special classifier for a character, use 個 GO⁴. 口 KOU³, mouth, the classifier for box.

110

PILING BOXES

小的、一個人抱一個

224 One man should carry one of the small boxes in his arms.

小的 SIAO³ DY², the small ones, same construction as in 223. 抱 BAO⁴, to carry in the arms, as a box, a baby, anything which one carries by putting his arms around it. In this sentence we have an excellent illustration of the freedom of use of the classifier 個 GO⁴; in No. 223 口 KOU¹, is used as the classifier for box; here 個 GO⁴ is used. Therefore 個 GO⁴ may be used in many cases where there is a special classifier.

趙興順、你把這個箱子、拷過去

225 Djao Hsin-Shwen, you carry this box over on your shoulder.

拷 LAO³, to carry on the shoulder, as one is apt to carry a hoe or a spade, or a gun, or a bag of grain.

好生、不要掉

226 Be careful, don't drop it.

好生 HAO³ SEN¹, be careful; see 165. 掉 DIAO⁴, to drop, to lose; very common.

怕打爛東西

227 I fear you would break things (in the box).

怕 PA⁴, fear, to fear; whole word is 害怕 HAI⁴ PA⁴, used much the same as in English. 打爛 DA³ LAN⁴, to break, to smash; *lit.*, to strike broken; very common.

把大箱子,放在這裡

228 Put the big boxes here.

平起放

229 Place it flat, or 'on the flat'.

平 PIN², level, flat, even.

這個拿來重起

230 Put this one on top of that.

拿來 LA² LAI², bring along. 重起 CHUNG² CHI³, to place on top, a most useful word. To place any article on top of any other article is 重起 CHUNG² CHI³. 重 is the ordinary character meaning 'heavy', and in this sense is pronounced DJUNG⁴.

這一口,可以側起放

231 This box you may place on its side.

側起 DZE² CHI³, sidewise, on the side; also means 'to incline' or 'to tip'.

底下一層,總要放大的一起

232 You must certainly put the big ones in the bottom layer.

底下 DI³ HSIA⁴, beneath, the bottom; it has the little word 在 DZAI⁴ understood. 層 TSEN², layer, story, tier. 總 DZUNG³, an emphatic particle. 一起 I² CHI³, a sort or kind. That is to say, 'the big sort'.

PILING BOXES

上頭幾層、耍重小的

233 You may pile the small ones up in the several layers above.

上頭 SHANG⁴ TOU², above; the character 在 DZAI⁴ is understood before the 上頭. 幾層 GI² TSEN², several layers. 重 CHUNG², to pile on top.

這一口、拖過來、立起放

234 Drag this one over and place it on end.

拖 TO¹, to drag, very similar to 拉 LA¹. 立起 LI² CHI³, to stand up, to place standing up.

這一口空箱子、呴倒放

235 Place this empty box upside down, (or mouth, downwards).

空 KUNG¹, empty. 不得空 BU² DE² KUNG⁴, I have no leisure, I have no time; note the change of tone in this sense. 呴倒 KOU² DAO³, to place mouth downwards; this character 呴 is only borrowed from its proper use to indicate this sound and tone. There seems to be no character for this word.

不對、不對

236 That is not right!

對 DUI⁴, right, correct. The duplication indicates emphasis.

翻過來、呴倒

237 Turn it over and place it mouth downwards.

翻 FAN¹, to turn over. The whole phrase 翻過來 FAN¹ GO⁴ LAI², is best translated by the very same phrase, 'to turn over'.

這個箱子、要打開

238 This box is to be opened.

打開 DA³ KAI¹, to open, whether the lid is locked, nailed, or not fastened at all. Very common.

面子在上頭、纔要得

239 The cover side should be up; *lit.*, The cover should be above, and then it will be satisfactory.

面子 MIEN⁴ DZ³, the cover, the upper or outside surface. 要得 YAO⁴ DE², satisfactory.

拿釘錘、給挾釘鉗來

240 Bring the hammer and the nail-puller.

釘錘 DIN¹ CHUE², hammer; commonly corrupted to DIN¹ CHWER². 挾釘鉗 GIA² DIN¹ TSIEN², a rather foreign term, which, however, is clearly self-explanatory; it is the 'pinch-nail-tongs'.

把釘子、一根一根的挾起來

241 Pull the nails out one by one.

釘子 DIN¹ DZ³, a nail, nails. The character 釘 DIN⁴, is also the common verb, to nail, but note that in this sense it is in the fourth tone. 根 GEN¹, a root, here used as the classifier for nail; it is the proper classifier for bench, 一根板櫈 I² GEN¹ BAN³ DEN⁴; and for cow, 一根牛 I² GEN¹ NIU². 一根一根的 I² GEN¹ I² GEN¹ DY², one by one,—usable with regard to anything for which 根 GEN¹ may be used as the classifier. 挾起來 GIA² CHI³ LAI², *lit.*, pinch up come, *i.e.* pull out, as by a nail-puller.

PILING BOXES

把細,不耍把板子橇爛了

242 Be careful, lest you break the board in prying it.

把細 BA³ SI⁴, be careful. See 165. 板子 BAN³ DZ³, a board. 橇爛了 CHIAO⁴ LAN⁴ LIAO³, pry broken, *i.e.* break in prying it.

釘子挾完了,沒有

243 Have you got all the nails out?

Lit., Have you pinched the nails completely or not? 完了 WAN² LIAO³, finished, completed, a very common term.

挾完了

244 I have them all out.

The personal pronoun 'I' is of course understood.

把蓋子,擱在一邊

245 Place the cover to one side.

蓋子 GAI⁴ DZ³, a cover. See 216. 在一邊 DZAI⁴ I² BIEN¹, at or on one side.

我要取東西

246 I want to take things out.

取 CHÜ³, to take away, to take out or down.

那裡還有個箱子

247 There is still another box there.

那裡 LA⁴ LI³, there, with 在 DZAI⁴ understood before it of course. If we change one tone, LA⁴ LI³, to LA³ LI³, the whole sentence is changed to 'Where is there another box?' 還 HAI², often read HWAN², still, yet, again, etc. 還有 HAI² YIU³, there still is. Note that the little character 一 I² is omitted before 個 GO⁴. This sort of omission often happens in free conversation.

重嗎,輕

248 Is it heavy or light?

重 DJUNG⁴, heavy; see 230. 輕 CHIN¹, light. The little character 嗎 MA¹, just indicates the interrogative, and is conveniently translated 'or'. This is an extremely common idiom; fix it in your mind.

不多重

249 It is not very heavy.

Lit., Not much heavy. See 203.

你一個人,抱不抱得起

250 Can you carry it alone?

一個人 I² GO⁴ REN², one individual, with the accent on the 個 GO⁴. 抱得起 BAO⁴ DE² CHI³, I can carry it; 抱不起 BAO⁴ BU² CHI³, I cannot carry it. The latter half of the sentence might have read: 'BAO⁴ DE² CHI³ MA¹, BAO⁴ BU² CHI³?' See 248 for idiom.

抱得起

251 I can carry it.

PILING BOXES

好, 抱起跟倒我來

252 Good! Pick it up and come along after me.

跟倒 GEN¹ DAO³, to follow; the most common term for this expression. 跟倒我來 GEN¹ DAO⁴, NGO³ LAI², *lit.*, follow me come, which is sufficiently clear.

就在那裡放倒

253 Put it down right there.

就 DZIU⁴, then; here appropriately translated 'just', 'exactly'.

輪起放

254 Place it on its edge (or narrow side).

輪 LEN² a wheel, to revolve; here 'edgewise', the same in its effect here as 側起 DZE² CHI³, in 231.

這個當頭爛了

255 This end is broken.

當頭 DANG⁴ TOU², the end board of a box.

底底到好

256 The bottom, however, is all right.

底底 DI³ DI³ or 底子 DI³ DZ³, bottom. 到 DAO⁴, here 'on the contrary'.

外頭還有箱子, 沒得

257 Are there still (any) boxes outside?

外頭 WAI⁴ TOU², outside, with 在 DZAI⁴, understood before it. 沒得 MU² DE¹, a corruption of 沒有 MU² YIU³, heard all over West China. The character 得 DE² in this phrase drops into almost any convenient tone, according to euphony. It is very frequently in the first tone, instead of the second.

沒得了

258 No. (There are none).

An extremely common phrase. The character 沒 MU² passes through all shades of MU², MO², and ME².

箱子,一把連一下,堆好了

259 The boxes are all piled up.

一把連一下 I² BA³ LIEN² I² HA⁴, 'all', emphatic and all-embracing. Common.

我們大家歇下氣

260 (Now) we shall all rest for a little.

大家 DA⁴ GIA¹, everybody, all. 歇 HSIE², to rest, to take a rest, to stay over night. 下 HSIA⁴, here HA⁴, with 一 I² understood before it. 歇氣 HSIE² CHI⁴, to rest one's breath, to rest; very common.

LESSON II. 第十一課

買轎子
Buying a Sedan Chair

買轎子

261 Buying a sedan chair.

買 MAI³, to buy. 轎子 GIAO⁴ DZ³, a sedan chair.

王長興,我要買一乘轎子

262 Wang Chang-Hsin, I want to buy a sedan chair.

This is in case you send your cook. You may prefer to go in person, which is quite all right. 一乘 I² CHEN², one piece; 乘 CHEN², the classifier for sedan chair.

先生要買二孤轆,嗎,三丁拐

263 Which do you want to buy, a two-man chair or a three-man chair?

二孤轆 ER⁴ GU¹ LU¹, a two-man chair; called 對班轎子 DUI⁴ BAN¹ GIAO⁴ DZ³ or DUI⁴ BER¹ GIAO⁴ DZ³, in many parts. 三丁拐 SAN¹ DIN¹ GWAI³, a three-man chair; constantly heard as as SAN¹ DIN¹ GWER³. Most of the characters

119

aside from the figures in these two names are rather difficult of explanation. But what is of much more importance is that the words are extremely common. One longs for the day when our Chinese friends will perhaps not emphasize CHARACTERS less, but will emphasize WORDS more.

兩樣都要

264 I want both kinds.

兩樣 LIANG³ YANG¼, two kinds; 都 DU¹, all; 要 YAO⁴, wanted.

我給你說一下, 你去講價

265 I shall tell you (what I want), and you (may) go and argue prices.

給你說 GE¹ NI³ SHO², tell you. 告訴 GAO⁴ SU⁴, is not used in West China. 講價 GIANG³ GIA⁴, argue prices. 講 GIANG³, is the common word to preach, explain, lecture; 價 GIA⁴, prices.

三丁拐, 要涼轎

266 I want the three-man chair to be an open chair.

涼轎 LIANG² GIAO⁴, *lit.*, cool chair, because not closed in.

二孤轕, 要舊樣子

267 I want the two-man chair to be of the old-fashioned sort.

舊 GIU⁴, old, applied to things. 樣子 YANG⁴ DZ³, sort, fashion.

BUYING A SEDAN CHAIR

兩乘、都要竹竿子

268 Both chairs should have bamboo poles.

兩乘 LIANG³ CHEN², two sedan chairs, using the classifier only. 竹 DJU², bamboo; 竿子 GAN¹ DZ³, poles. Note the use of 都 DU¹, all, both, thus making sure that the 兩 LIANG³ includes both chairs!

竹竿子、要刷黑搓油

269 The bamboo poles I want painted black and oiled.

刷 SHWA², to brush; 黑 HE², black; 搓 TSO¹, to rub with the hands; 油 YIU², oil. Oil is rubbed on with silk waste in place of a brush.

傳子給杵皮、要青棡

270 I want the shoulder-piece and upright to be of oak.

傳子 CHWAN² DZ³, the heavy piece of wood resting on the shoulders of the two men who carry the front end of a three-man chair. 杵皮 CHU³ PI², the lighter piece of wood used to support the front end of the three-man chair while the men change shoulders. 青棡 CHIN¹ GANG¹, oak wood or tree. 給 GE¹, and. If you are in need of a word for 'and'—and most of us foreigners are—here we have the best word in Chinese spoken language. It has also the common meanings 'to give', 'to pay', but is constantly used as 'and'.

兩個都要上顏色、搓油

271 I want both to be colored and oiled.

顏色 YEN² SE², color; 上顏色 SHANG⁴ YEN² SE², to put on coloring.

擔肩子給千斤，要結實

272. I want the cross-pieces between the ends of the chair-poles to be strong.

擔肩子 DAN⁴ GIEN¹ DZ³, the cross-piece which is made of bamboo, and which is bound to the chair-poles by string or rope. *Lit.*, 擔 DAN⁴, a burden, or DAN¹, first tone, to bear a burden; 肩子 GIEN¹ DZ³, shoulder. 千斤 TSIEN¹ GIN¹, the cross-piece made of wood, not bamboo, mortised into the front ends of the poles of a three-man chair. *Lit.*, 千斤 TSIEN¹ GIN¹, thousand catties. 結實 GIE² SHĬ², firm, strong.

紉使棕繩包皮

273. The rope loops are to be made of bark rope covered with leather.

紉 KOU¹, the pair of rope loops by means of which the three-man chair is suspended in front; a character borrowed for this purpose. 使 SHĬ³, use; 棕繩 DZUNG¹ SHWEN², palm-bark rope. 包 BAO¹, to wrap up; 皮 PI², skin, leather; *i.e.*, leather wrapped.

油布、雨簾、兩乘都要

274. Both chairs should have rain curtains made of oiled cotton.

油布 YIU² BU⁴, oiled cotton; 雨簾 YÜ³ LIEN², rain curtains. Note the regular appearance of the character 都 DU¹ after numbers: 兩乘都要 LIANG³ CHEN² DU¹ YAO⁴, both chairs all want.

涼轎、格外要一套紗簾

275. The open chair requires, in addition, a set of curtains made of finely split bamboo.

BUYING A SEDAN CHAIR

格外 GE² WAI⁴, in addition, besides; very common. 一套 I² TAO⁴, a set. 紗 SHA¹, *lit.*, gauze; used for the fine bamboo curtains as well.

舊樣轎子，要一套玻璃窻子

276 The old-style sedan chair requires a set of glass windows.

舊樣 GIU⁴ YANG⁴, old style or sort; 玻璃 BO¹LI², glass; 窻子 TSANG¹ DZ³, windows; properly pronounced CHWANG¹ DZ³, but the corruption or localism TSANG¹ DZ³, is more or less general over West China.

又要一套紗窻

277 It also requires a set of gauze windows.

又 YIU⁴, also. 紗窻 SHA¹ TSANG¹, gauze (or any fine mesh stuff) windows.

要一套紬簾子

278 I want a set of silk curtains.

紬子 CHOU² DZ³, the general name for all kinds of silk.

裏頭要安花瓶、鏡子

279 Inside I want placed a flower vase and a mirror.

裏頭 LI³ TOU², inside, with 在 DZAI⁴, understood before it. 安 NGAN¹, to place. 花瓶 HWA¹ PIN², flower bottle or vase. 鏡子 GIN⁴ DZ³, a mirror.

舊樣轎子、又要花洋緞墊子

280 The old style chair also requires cushions covered with flowered sateen, (foreign).

花洋緞 HWA¹ YANG² DWAN⁴, flowered foreign satin, which we commonly call sateen. 墊子 DIEN⁴ DZ³, cushions. See 204.

天棚、靠背、帽架、都要

281 The "heavenly tent", back-support, hat rack,—all are required.

天棚 TIEN¹ PUNG², lit., heavenly tent, the little shelf placed under the forward end of the roof of the chair. 靠背 KAO⁴ BEI⁴, lit., 'lean back', the back support inside the chair. 帽架 MAO⁴ GIA⁴, hat rack, placed under and attached close up to the roof of the chair.

舊樣轎子、還要一個大雨幃

282 The old-style chair also requires a big rain curtain.

雨幃 YÜ³ WEI², rain curtain, which is put around three sides of the chair in case of rain.

兩乘轎子、都用瓦頂

283 Both chairs are to have tile tops.

瓦頂 WA³ DIN³, tile tops, i.e. tile-shaped roofs. These are lighter and cheaper than the more elaborate style.

請他用好洋布作油布

284 Ask him to use good foreign cotton to make the oil-cloths.

BUYING A SEDAN CHAIR

洋布 YANG² BU⁴, foreign cotton, *i.e.* cotton cloth.

那個稀布不行

285 That very thin cloth will not do.

稀 HSI¹, thin, open, sleazy; 稀飯 HSI¹ FAN⁴, thin rice, *i.e.* porridge, this is the name ordinarily used by foreigners for porridge. 不行 BU² HSIN², will not do, will not work; a very common phrase, most useful for every-day purposes.

凉轎的坐位,要拱起編

286 The seat of the open chair is to be plaited in a convex shape.

坐位 DZO⁴ WEI⁴, a seat, *lit.*, sit place. 拱起 GUNG³ CHI³, to bow or bulge up, to be convex. 編 BIEN¹, to plait, to weave. The seat is of plaited cane or rattan.

不編平的

287 It is not to be plaited level.

Lit., Not plait level. Then why the character 的 DY²? Because the complete sentence would have about three more characters, beginning, 坐位是 DZO⁴ WEI⁴ SHI⁴, seat is..... To make this sentence absolutely clear we must add that 坐位 DZO⁴ WEI⁴, is again understood after the 的 DY². The perfect sentence would then read 坐位是不編平的坐位 the seat is a not-plaited-level seat.

王長興,你去講一下,回來說

288 Wang Chang-Hsin, you go and argue a while, and come back and report.

回來 HWEI² LAI², to return; 轉來 DJWAN³ LAI², same meaning exactly, and possibly a little more used. 說 SHO², speak, say, report.

我今下午去

289 I will go this afteroon.

Lit., I to-day afternoon go.

我去了來咯

290 (Wang reports) I have been and come back.

Lit., I went came. 了 LIAO³, sign of past tense; 咯 LO², exactly the same as the last; perhaps originally a corruption of 了 LIAO³.

掌櫃說，两乘轎子，要三十塊錢

291 The proprietor says that he wants thirty dollars for the two chairs.

掌櫃 DJANG³ GWEI⁴, proprietor of a shop, a term pretty well limited to Chengtu. In other places mostly 老板 LAO³ BAN³. 三十塊錢 SAN¹ SHI² KWAI³ TSIEN², *lit.*, thirty pieces money, thirty *i.e.* dollars.

我給了他二十五塊

292 I offered him twenty-five dollars.

Lit., I gave him $25.00, which is the usual way of saying, 'I offered him $25.00'.

他沒有賣

293 (But) he would not sell.

BUYING A SEDAN CHAIR

That is to say he did not take up my offer. The conjunction is almost always omitted in such a case; I have included it in brackets.

我諳要二十六七塊，纔買得倒

294 I think it will take $26.00 or $27.00 to buy (the two chairs).

諳 NGAN², to think, guess, conjecture. Note the way we say '$26.00 or $27.00', 二十六七塊 ER⁴ SHÏ² LU² TSI² KWAI³ ; the 'or' is understood, as also the word for 'dollars' at the end. 纔買得倒 TSAI² MAI³ DE² DAO³, then, and not till then, they can be bought.

可以去還他二十六塊錢

295 You may go and offer him $26.00.

還 HWAN², to offer; same character as elsewhere read HAI², with the meaning 'still', 'yet', etc.

LESSON 12. 第十二課

坐轎子
Sedan Chair Riding

坐轎子
296 Sedan chair riding.

Lit., Sitting in a sedan chair, which is the Chinese way of saying 'riding in a sedan chair', or 'travelling by sedan chair.'

看門頭，喊兩個甩手來
297 Gateman, call two chair-bearers.

看 KAN⁴, to see, to watch; 門 MEN², gate, door; 頭 TOU², head; 'watch-gate-head', = gateman. The third character is often corrupted to TER², and the accent is largely on the TER², KAN⁴ MEN² TER²! One's gateman may be so addressed; or any gateman whose name one does not know. It is better, however, for one to use his own gateman's name, either with his HAO⁴, or, if the gateman is fifty years of age or over, using the style DA⁴ YE², as DJANG¹ DA⁴ YE². 喊 HAN³, to call; used for any servant, or for any laborer or any one of that class, not for a teacher. 甩手 SHWAI³ SHOU³, *lit.,* swing hands, *i.e.* empty-handed men. This pre-supposes that one owns his own sedan chair.

先生過那裡去
298 Where are you going? (Asked by the chair-bearers).

SEDAN CHAIR RIDING

過 GO⁴, to go, to pass, to go over; the whole verb is 過去 GO⁴ CHÜ⁴, a combination of the two words meaning to go, with the word 那裏 LA³ LI³, interrogative 'where', inserted between. This is perhaps the commonest method of asking where one is going.

要過四聖祠去

299 I want to go to Sī Shen Tsī.

This may be translated, 'I am going to Sī Shen Tsī'. The name is that of a street; in Chengtu the premises of each Mission is rarely known by the Mission name, but by the name of the street.

單邊、嗎、來回

300 Is this to be a round trip or a single trip?

單邊 DAN¹ BIEN¹, single side; 嗎 MA¹, or, and sign of interrogative; 來回 LAI² HWEI², come return, *i.e.* round trip. This extremely brief form of expression is much used, and is perfectly understood, in just this sense.

來回

301 (It is to be a) round trip.

把轎子升起

302 Tip the chair up.

升起 SHEN¹ CHI³, raise up, elevate; the common expression always used when one wishes the chairmen to tip the chair up from behind in order that one may step easily over the front pole, into the space between the poles, and so enter the chair. If one is standing beside the chair ready to enter, the first three characters may be omitted.

升平

303　Let the chair down to the level.

　　升 SHEN[1], elevate; 平 PIN[2], level; this is one of the beautiful inconsistencies of this language. Of course it can be explained; in the first sentence, 升 SHEN[1], refers to the back end of the poles; in this sentence, to the front end!

抬起走

304　Start!

　　Lit., Lift up walk, *i.e.* pick up the chair and start. 走 DZOU[3], walk, go.

倒右手拐

305　Turn the corner to the right.

　　倒 DAO[3], to fall over, to turn a corner; 右 YIU[4], right; 手 SHOU[3], hand; 拐 GWAI[3], corner, to kidnap. This is the character used in the name of the three-man chair, see 263.

左手倒拐

306　Turn the corner to the left.

　　Either form of expression, 305 or 306 is good, and they are about equally used, I think.

站倒下

307　Stand still a moment.

　　站 DJAN[4], to stand; 倒 DAO[3], implying completed action; 下 HA[4], a little, a moment. The last is a character borrowed for this purpose; its usual meaning is 'beneath', and it is pronounced HSIA[4]. Note the omission of the 一 I[2], before 下 HA[4]. It is not at all wrong to insert it, but this form 站倒下 is as usually spoken.

SEDAN CHAIR RIDING

走

308 Go on.

    This expression is much used in this sense, just the single character 走 DZOU³, often repeated, 走 走 DZOU³, DZOU³, by a member or members of a group who have stopped to look at something on the street, or who have come into a chapel together. One says 走 DZOU³, and another answers 走 走 DZOU³, DZOU³, and the whole company of four or five or more rise and leave together.

快点走

309 Walk a little faster.

    快 KWAI⁴, fast; 点 DIEN³, a little; *lit.*, 'fast a little', but really 'a little faster'. Very common.

提 倒

310 Put the chair down.

    This is the expression to use when you wish your chair put down so you may get out, and is usable under all circumstances and conditions.

把簾子揭起

311 Take off the curtains.

    揭起 DZIE² CHI³, or 揭開 DZIE² KAI¹, to open, to take off, as a cover to a box or a dish. 簾子 LIEN² DZ³, curtains.

把下簾揭開

312 Take off the lower curtain.

下 HSIA⁴, beneath, lower ; 簾 LIEN², curtain. Note that when the 簾 LIEN², gets another word before it, the adjective 下 HSIA⁴, there is no longer the same necessity for the 子 DZ³. The real object of the 子 DZ³ is to make the word into a dissyllable, and this is secured by the addition of 下 HSIA⁴.

把轎子升起

313 Tip the chair up.

Same as 302, only that in this case you are inside the poles, and wish to step out.

先生耍躭擱好久纔走

314 How long will it be before you leave ?

躭擱 DAN¹ GO², to delay, to hinder, to stop work ; a very common phrase used by the servant when he wishes to be let away from his work for an hour or a day. Here the meaning is, 'How long will you delay (or stay) before going ?' 好久 HAO³ GIU³, how long (in time) ? Very common. But it is declarative as well as interrogative. This 擱 GO² of 躭擱 DAN¹ GO² is the same character as we use for KO⁴, to put, to place, only that the latter is pronounced with a different sound and different tone. See 201 and 320.

躭擱一點鐘

315 I am going to stay an hour.

一點鐘 I² DIEN³ DJUNG¹, one hour, one o'clock ; *lit.*, one point o'clock. How do you distinguish between these two meanings ? It is difficult ; you do it by the other part of the remark and by the conversation generally. Judging by this phrase alone, it is impossible.

SEDAN CHAIR RIDING

抬轎子的,走咯

316 Chair-bearers! We are going.

　　抬轎子的 TAI² GIAO⁴ DZ³ DY², carry-chair-men, with 人 REN² understood after 的 DY²; *i.e.* chair-bearers. This is your call to the chair coolies to come, because you wish to start. 走咯 DZOU³ LO², *lit.*, gone; that is to say, 'I am starting'. This expression differs from the single character 走 DZOU³, in being more emphatic, in expressing one's own determination to go, rather than an exhortation to them to start. 走 DZOU³, is used among equals, 走咯 DZOU³ LO² by the master to his employees.

天要下雨,掛不掛雨幛

317 It is going to rain, shall we put on the rain curtain?

　　This is said by the chairmen. *Lit.*, 'The sky is about to drop rain'. 下雨 HSIA⁴ YŬ³, and 落雨 LO² YŬ³, are the two common expressions meaning 'to rain', 'it is raining', 下 HSIA⁴, and 落 LO², both meaning to drop, to fall down. 掛 GWA⁴, to hang up, as a curtain, a hat, a garment. 掛不掛 GWA⁴ BU² GWA⁴, hang up not hang up, *i.e.* shall we hang up?

可以掛起

318 You may put it on.

攏了屋頭

319 We have arrived home.

　　攏 LUNG³, to arrive; 攏了 LUNG³ LIAO³, we have arrived; 屋頭 WU² TOU², said by some to be the best term in Chinese for 'home', although not having anything like the wealth of meaning attached to the English word. 屋 WU², is room, family, home; 頭 TOU², is the last word of the three-character phrase 在裏頭 DZAI⁴ LI³ TOU², inside, and has the same meaning as the whole phrase.

把轎子擱好

320 Put the chair away properly.

擱 KO⁴, to put, to place. Why not have used 撿好 GIEN³ HAO³, as in 152 and 177? So we might, only that the sedan chair seems rather bulky to be 'put away' like a cloth or a pail!

王長興可以給轎錢

321 Wang Chang-Hsin, you may pay the chair money.

給 GE¹, to give, to hand to; to offer; also 'and', see 270 and 292. 轎 GIAO⁴, chair; 錢 TSIEN², money, cash.

給好多錢、先生

322 How much shall I pay? (Asked by the cook).

給 GE¹, give; 好多 HAO³ DO¹, how much; 錢 TSIEN², cash. 先生 SIEN¹ SEN¹, Teacher, Mr. Sir, but better not translated here.

照規矩給錢、就是了

323 Pay according to the custom, simply.

照 DJAO⁴, according to; 規矩 GWEI¹ GÜ³, custom, rules, regulations; 就是了 DZIU⁴ SHÏ⁴ LIAO³, 'simply', 'and that's all there is about it'. This phrase of three characters is extremely common, and extremely handy for finishing off a sentence in this way. Like most of the rest of the

SEDAN CHAIR RIDING

Chinese language, it is very difficult to learn from books; but by listening closely, and by beginning as soon as possible to make use of it, one seems to grow into the knowledge of it.

添不添茶錢

324 Shall I add tea money? (Asked by the cook).

添 TIEN[1], to add; 茶 CHA[2], tea; 錢 TSIEN[2], money.

路爛,可以添茶錢,各人六個

325 When the road is bad, you may add tea money, six cash to each man.

的時侯 DY[2] SHI[2] HOU[4], when, is understood after the first two characters. 路 LU[4], road, street; 爛 LAN[4], muddy, broken, smashed; 各 GO[2], each, every; 六個 LU[2] GO[4], six (cash, understood).

LESSON 13. 第十三課

坐轎子出遠門
Travelling by Sedan Chair

坐轎子出遠門

326 Travelling by sedan chair.

出 CHU², to go out; 遠 YUEN³, distant; 門 MEN², gate, door. Therefore 'to take a long journey by chair'.

王長興我要出門

327 Wang Chang-Hsin, I am going on a journey.

我 NGO³, I; 要 YAO⁴, am about to; 出門 CHU² MEN², to go on a journey. Lit., to go out of the gate, the city gate, presumably.

先生過那裡去

328 Where are you going?

See 298.

要過仁壽

329 I am going to Jenshow.

I want to go to Jenshow, I am about to go to Jenshow, would be equally good translations.

TRAVELLING BY SEDAN CHAIR

可以去喊三個肛手兩個挑夫

330 You may go and call three chair-bearers and two load coolies.

See 297. 挑夫 TIAO¹ FU¹, carry-with-shoulder-pole men, load coolies. Also commonly called 脚子 GIO² DZ³. 挑 TIAO¹, to carry by means of a pole across the shoulders.

你去講一下價回來說

331 You go and argue prices for a little, and come back and report.

See 288. 價 GIA⁴, price; used as a dissyllable as 價錢 GIA⁴ TSIEN².

王長興回來的時候說

332 When Wang Chang-Hsin returned, he said

他要六百五十個錢一站

333 he wants 650 cash a stage.

The cost of chair-bearers and load coolies is usually reckoned by the stage, and this varies from 80 to 120 *li* a day. 一站 I² DJAN⁴, a stage, one stage. Same word as we had in 307, meaning to stand still.

少了不去

334 For less than this, they will not go.

少 SHAO³, less.

你問過幾個舖子

335　At how many shops did you ask?

　　Lit., You asked how many shops? 問 WEN⁴, to ask; 過 GO⁴, sign of past tense; 幾個 GI³ GO⁴, how many, especially when the number is under ten; 舖子 PU⁴ DZ³, shops. It is quite proper in China to ask prices in at least three shops, in order to form a judgment as to the real price.

問過兩三處

336　I asked in two or three places.

　　兩三處 LIANG³ SAN¹ CHU⁴, two three places, *i.e.* two or three places.

有喊八百錢一站

337　Some asked 800 cash a stage;

　　有 YIU³, has either 些 HSIE¹, or 的 DY² understood after it, and means 'some shops, or people'; 喊 HAN³, to call, to ask a price; there is included in this word a little of the idea of arguing or haggling prices; that is to say, more was 'called' than they really expected to receive. See 297.

有喊七百錢一站

338　some asked 700 cash a stage;

只有這一處說的這麼合式

339　only this one place talked as satisfactorily as this.

TRAVELLING BY SEDAN CHAIR

只 GĬ³, only; 有 YIU³, there was; 這一處 DJE⁴ I² CHU⁴, this one place; 說的 SHO² DY², spoke, talked; 這麼 DJE⁴ MO³, thus, in this way; 合式 HO² SHĬ⁴, satisfactory, suitable, agreeable. The last is a common word, and very useful; it is applied especially to things.

好、使得

340 Good! That will do.

使得 SHĬ³ DE², that will do, "can do" in pidgin English; very similar to 要得 YAO⁴ DE², but the latter is stronger, much.

可以把這五百錢拿去交定錢

341 You may take this 500 cash and give it as earnest money.

拿去 LA² CHÜ⁴, take away, as opposed to 'bring'. 交 GIAO¹, to hand over, to deliver, a very useful word for everyday purposes. 定錢 DIN⁴ TSIEN², 'fix' money, = earnest money.

王長興、這一下子同我一路來

342 Now then, Wang Chang-Hsin, you come with me;

這一下子 DJE⁴ I² HA⁴ DZ³, now, now then; see 215, 220. 同我一路 TUNG² NGO³ I² LU⁴, 'with me one road', along with me; 來 LAI², come.

我們到零貨房頭去

343 We will go to the store room.

我們 NGO³ MEN², we; 到 DAO⁴, to; 零貨房 LIN² HO⁴ FANG², store room, lit., 零 LIN², odds and ends; 貨 HO⁴, goods; 房 FANG², room, house. 頭 TOU², as in 319, part of the three character phrase 在裏頭 DZAI⁴ LI³ TOU², meaning 'inside'. 去 CHÜ⁴, to go.

這一挑篾簍拿出去

344 This pair of bamboo baskets you may take out.

A pair of containers used by the carrying coolie is always called 一挑 I² TIAO¹; not a 'man-load', but what is used in carrying a man-load. 篾 MI², strips of bamboo; 簍 LOU³, basket; 拿出去 LA² CHU² CHÜ⁴, 'take go out go', which effectually disposes of all possible ambiguity! I have called these 'baskets', because the heavy bamboo box used for baggage is called 篾箱 MI² SIANG¹, not 篾簍 MI² LOU³.

這挑篾箱也要拿出去

345 This pair of bamboo boxes is also to be taken out.

篾箱 MI² SIANG¹, bamboo boxes. 也 YE³, also.

兩挑都要抖乾淨

346 Both pair (of baskets are to be shaken clean (of dust).

抖 TOU³, to shake, as a rug or a tablecloth; to tremble, as from a fit of ague.

拿報紙糊裏子

347 Take a newspaper and paste it in as a lining.

TRAVELLING BY SEDAN CHAIR

報 BAO⁴, newspaper, magazine; 紙 GI³, paper; 糊 HU², to paste, corrupted very generally in West China to FU¹. Note the change of tone as well as change of sound. This change from HU² to FU² is common to a great many characters of this group, although the tone does not usually change. 裏子 LI³ DZ³, lining, as the lining of a garment.

要攪漿子把紙糊穩

348 You are to make paste, and paste the paper firmly.

攪 GIAO³, to stir; 漿子 GIANG⁴ DZ³, paste made with flour; 攪漿子 GIAO³ GIANG⁴ DZ³, to make paste. 穩 WEN³, firm; see 202, 203, 205.

糊起了就拿出去晒

349 When you have (the lining) pasted, take (them) out and sun (them).

'When' is understood.

多買幾根繩子

350 (I want you to) buy a good number of ropes.

多 DO¹, much, many; 買 MAI³, buy; 幾 GI³, several; 根 GEN¹, a root, the classifier for ropes; 繩子 SHWEN² DZ³, a rope or ropes, cords, strings. 索子 SO² DZ³, is another very common word for ropes, and usually implies one of larger size than 繩子 SHWEN² DZ³.

The idiom of this sentence is peculiar. There is a distinct idea of comparison in the 多買 DO¹ MAI³; here, it is that several more ropes should be bought than usual for such a trip.

買棕繩子纔好

351 It will be better to buy the bark ropes.

又可以買幾根細麻索子

352　You may also buy several fine hemp ropes.

　　細 SI⁴, fine, as opposed to coarse 粗 TSU¹. 麻 MA², hemp; 索子 SO² DZ³, ropes.

這根挑子作伙食挑子

353　This load we shall make the food load.

　　挑子 TIAO¹ DZ³, a man-load, baggage; 作 DZO², to be, to act as, "we shall make"; 伙食 HO³ SHI̊², food supplies, the usual term.

一頭少裝十幾斤

354　Put ten odd catties less (than custom) into one of the baskets (ends),

　　一 I², one; 頭 TOU², end, *i.e.* basket; 少 SHAO³, less, few; 裝 DJWANG¹, to fill, to put in; 十幾斤 SHI̊² GI³ GIN¹, over ten and under twenty catties.

好在面上搭床架子

355　so we can place a folding cot on top.

　　好 HAO³, good, convenient, "so that it will be convenient to"; 在面上 DZAI⁴ MIEN⁴ SHANG⁴, on top, on the surface; 搭 DA², place, lay; 床 CHWANG², bed; 架子 GIA⁴ DZ³, frame. This 搭 DA², to place, differs from 擱 KO⁴ and 放 FANG⁴ in that the last two words are general in their meaning, whereas 搭 DA² usually means to place an article on a special kind of a support, as a towel on a towel-rack, a garment over the back of a chair; it might be translated 'to suspend', 'to hang over'.

TRAVELLING BY SEDAN CHAIR

每一頭頂多裝四十斤

356 In each end pack a maximum of forty catties.

每 MEI³, each; 一頭 I² TOU², an end, *i.e.* end of a load, a basket; 頂多 DIN³ DO¹, the very most, the maximum; 裝 DJWANG¹, to fill, to pack. 斤 GIN¹, the catty or Chinese pound.

每一挑八十斤爲限,少得,多不得

357 For each load eighty catties is the limit; you may put in less but not more.

爲 WEI², as; when this character is part of 因爲 YIN¹ WEI⁴, it is in the fourth tone, and means 'because'. Not infrequently it is met with alone in the fourth tone, meaning 'because'. 限 HSIEN⁴, a limit, to limit; 少得 SHAO³ DE², lessen can, *i.e.* 'it may be lessened' using the word 少 SHAO³ as a verb; 多不得 DO¹ BU² DE², increased not can, *i.e.* 'may not be increased', using 多 DO¹, as a verb, 'to increase'.

盡都耍過秤

358 All (the baskets) are to be weighed.

盡 DZIN⁴, all, entirely; 都 DU¹, all; two 'alls' coming together surely make the meaning clear! 過秤 GO⁴ CHEN⁴, *lit.*, 'to pass the scales', *i.e.* 'to be weighed'. 秤 CHEN⁴ in this tone = 'scales'; 稱 CHEN¹, to weigh.

王長興,明天起身過仁壽

359 Wang Chang-Hsin, to-morrow we shall start for Jenshow.

起身 CHI³ SHEN¹, to start on a journey; *lit.*, start body.

今天可以去招呼那個二掌櫃

360　You may go to-day to call that sub-manager.

招呼 DJAO¹ FU¹, to call, to beckon; 二掌櫃 ER⁴ DJANG³ GWEI⁴, No. 2 proprietor or manager, sub-manager.

給他說明天天亮要人

361　Tell him that we want the men to-morrow at daylight.

給他說 GE¹ TA¹ SHO², tell him, see 265. 明天 MIN² TIEN¹, to-morrow; 天亮 TIEN¹ LIANG⁴, dawn, *lit.*, 'day light'; 要人 YAO⁴ REN², want men.

我們未亮就起來收拾挑子

362　We shall get up before dawn, to get the loads into shape.

未亮 WEI⁴ LIANG⁴, not yet light; 起來 CHI³ LAI², to get up, to rise in the morning; 收拾 SHOU¹ SHI², to put to rights, to repair, as a house; 挑子 TIAO¹ DZ³, the loads.

先生要吃早飯纔走嗎

363　Do you want to take breakfast before starting?

Lit., Teacher want eat early rice then go? 早飯 DZAO³ FAN⁴, breakfast. 纔走 TSAI² DZOU³, and then go. 嗎 MA¹, sign of interrogative.

TRAVELLING BY SEDAN CHAIR

是的,要在屋裏吃早飯

364　Yes, I want to take breakfast at home.

　　是的 SHĪ⁴ DY², yes; but 'yes' in Chinese does not seem to carry very strong conviction; it needs the affirmative of the remark added, to make sure. 在屋裏 DZAI⁴ WU² LI³, at home; 吃 CHĪ², to eat.

上路的時候纔少躭擱

365　And then we shall be subject to less delay when we get on the road.

　　上路 SHANG⁴ LU⁴, to go on the road, to actually get out on the road as we start on the journey. 纔 TSAI², then; the use of this character here indicates at once a connection with the previous sentence. 少躭擱 SHAO³ DAN¹ GO², less delay.

LESSON 14. 第十四課

上路
On the Road

上路
366 On the road.

Lit., Going on the road.

王長興、挑子裝歸一了沒有
367 Wang Chang-Hsin, are the loads all properly packed?

The phrase 歸一 GWEI¹ I², carries something of the idea of 'all' in its meaning of completeness.

裝歸一了
368 They are all packed properly.

好、這一下子要鎖倒
369 Good; now then they should be locked.

鎖 SO³, to lock, a lock; 鎖倒 SO³ DAO³, to lock up.

ON THE ROAD

箱子一把連都鎖好了

370 The boxes are all safely locked up.

箱子 SIANG¹ DZ³, boxes; 一把連 I² BA³ LIEN², all, see 259; 都 DU¹, all, another instance of two 'alls' placed together. 好了 HAO³ LIAO³, gives the idea of 'safely', as well as that of completion.

可以喊他們擔挑子的進來

371 You may call the load coolies in.

擔挑子的 DAN¹ TIAO¹ DZ³ DY², with 人 REN² understood after it = carry-load-men, *i.e.* load coolies. Why not have used the characters 那些 LA⁴ HSIE¹, 'those' instead of 他們 TA¹ MEN²? One can only answer that the demonstrative adjectives 這 DJE⁴ and 那 LA⁴, especially when made into the plural by the addition of 些 HSIE¹, do not seem to sound very well when applied to persons. The two characters 他們 TA¹ MEN², as in this sentence, might well be translated 'those', although they are well left untranslated, as I have done. This is a very common construction. 進來 DZIN⁴ LAI², come in.

把索子套好

372 Put the ropes around carefully.

套 TAO⁴, to loop over or around, as a rope around a box or parcel. 好 HAO³, carries the idea of carefulness and completeness.

先生這根挑子重了,擔不起

373 This load is too heavy, we can't carry it.

重 了 DJUNG⁴ LIAO³, too heavy; 擔 DAN¹, to carry with shoulder-pole; 擔不起 DAN¹ BU² CHI³, (I) cannot carry it; *lit.*, carry-not-come up.

不得重、盡都稱過的

374 It cannot be too heavy, every one of them has been weighed.

The phrase 不得重 BU² DE² DJUNG⁴, has 了 LIAO³ understood after it; hence 'It cannot be *too* heavy'. 稱 CHEN¹, to weigh; 過 GO⁴, sign of past tense.

每一頭不得過四十斤

375 Each basket is not over 40 catties.

Lit., Each end cannot pass over 40 catties.

擔起走、擔起走

376 Get started, get started with the loads.

擔起走 DAN¹ CHI³ DZOU³, *lit.*, lift up on your shoulders, start, go. A common way of urging the load coolies to make a start.

慢點、我給你們說個話

377 Wait a minute, I want to say a word to you.

慢點 MAN⁴ DIEN³, slow a little, *i.e.* wait a minute; 等一下 DENG³ I² HA⁴, differs from this by being used in the sense of 'await (my pleasure) a little'; await rather than wait. The word 'want' is not expressed in Chinese; the thought is so rapid that it is not needed. 話 HWA⁴, words; here a 'word', in exactly the same sense as the English word.

ON THE ROAD

你們兩個擔挑子的、回回都要同三個抬轎子的在一處吃飯

378 You two load coolies must eat every time in the same place with the three chair-bearers.

回回 HWEI² HWEI², every time; 都 DU¹, all, joined with the HWEI² HWEI², to make absolutely sure of the inclusiveness of the order. 同 TUNG², with, together with; 三個抬轎子的 SAN¹ GO⁴ TAI² GIAO⁴ DZ³ DY², three carry-chair-men, the 人 REN² understood. 在一處 DZAI⁴ I² CHU⁴, in in one place; 吃飯 CHI² FAN⁴, to take food.

要常常跟倒轎子一路

379 You must always keep right along with the chair-~~bearers~~.

常常 SHANG² SHANG², always; the more commonly used expression for 'always' is 長行 CHANG² HSIN². 跟倒 GEN¹ DAO³, to follow; but here this phrase combined with the 一路 I² LU⁴, one road, *i.e.* travelling together.

把話聽清楚沒有

380 Do you understand clearly what I have said?

聽 TIN¹, to hear. There are very very few Chinese characters that may be pronounced at will in either of two tones, but this is one. It is both first and fourth; and yet conditions of euphony have an effect on it, determining whether it shall be the one or the other, in many instances. 清楚 TSIN¹ TSU³, clear, plain; very common and very useful.

聽清楚了

381 We have heard clearly.

好、擔起走

382 Good, now start off.

王長興、把這洗臉盆撿在海底下

383 Wang Chang-Hsin, put this washbasin under the seat of the chair.

洗臉盆 SI³ LIEN³ PEN², *lit.,* wash face basin. 撿 GIEN³, put away; 在海底下 DZAI⁴ HAI³ DI³ HSIA⁴, under the seat of the chair; *lit.,* 'at the bottom of the sea'! See 281 for the "heavenly tent". Chair-bearers are fond of high-sounding names.

還有這個小篼篼、雨鞋給傘

384 Here are also this small basket, my rubbers and umbrella.

篼篼 DOU¹ DOU¹, basket, a general name. 雨鞋 YÜ³ HAI², rubbers; *lit.,* 'rain shoes'. 給 GE¹, and; see 270. 傘 SAN³, umbrella; also called 撐花 TSEN¹ HWA¹, corrupted to TSEN¹ HWER¹. This last expression is especially used by those who are superstitious about using the word SAN³, with its suggestion of scattering, 散.

都要撿在轎子頭

385 All are to be put into the chair.

在 DZAI⁴.... 頭 TOU², has 裏 LI³ understood between: in, inside.

ON THE ROAD

鋪蓋拿去擱轎子

386 Take this pugai and cushion the chair with it.

Note the opening of the sentence with this most important word in the sentence, 鋪蓋 PU¹ GAI⁴. (This is one of the few Chinese words which we may be forgiven for incorporating into our English, because of the lack of any reasonable equivalent). 擱 BA⁴, to cushion the chair; to spread one's bed, as in 擱鋪 BA⁴ PU¹, an extremely common phrase.

這一下子門門歸一了，抬起走

387 Now then, everything is in order, let us make a start.

門門 MEN² MEN², everything; *lit.*, 'sort sort' 抬起走 TAI² CHI³ DZOU³, start! Said to chair-bearers; *lit.*, lift-up-go.

先生、右竿子頓點

388 The right pole is a little weak,

軟 RWAN³, weak; also 爬 PA¹, more used.

請巴倒左手坐

389 will you please sit close up to the left side.

This is the continuation and completion of the previous sentence. 巴倒 BA¹ DAO³, to get close to, to rest on; 左手 DZO³ SHOU³, left hand; 坐 DZO⁴, to sit.

提倒、我走上坡

390 Put the chair down, and I will walk up the hill.

There is no 'and' expressed; it is not needed. 上 SHANG⁴, to go up; 坡 PO¹, a hill, an incline, a bank. These two words 上坡 SHANG⁴ PO¹, are exactly what one says when he wants to go ashore from a boat.

轎子提倒，我要坐

391 Put the chair down, I want to ride.

Note the beginning of the sentence with the most important word, the noun 轎子 GIAO⁴ DZ³.

只要你們平路走得快

392 If you will only travel fast on the level parts of the road,

只 GÎ³, only; 平路 PIN² LU⁴, level road; 快 KWAI⁴, fast.

我讓轎的時侯多

393 I shall be willing to walk much.

This is the continuation of the previous sentence. *Lit.,* I yield chair times numerous. That is to say, I shall be pleased to relieve you of my weight many times. Note the entire absence of any conjunction between the two halves of the whole sentence; it does not seem necessary to use one in the English however. Note also this new use of the now familiar phrase 的時侯 DY² SHÎ² HOU⁴; here it can scarcely be translated 'when', unless one were to say, 'The times when I yield the chair (will be) numerous'.

站倒，打個穩杵

394 Stand still; support the chair on the upright piece.

ON THE ROAD

打個穩杵 DA³ GO⁴ WEN³ CHU³, strike a firm upright piece; *i.e.* allow the front end of the chair to rest on the upright stick for a time, instead of on the men's shoulders. In case it is a four-man chair, the whole weight of the chair may be supported for a time on the two uprights.

掉頭子，請你給我買十個錢的花生

395 Front carrier, will you please buy ten cash worth of peanuts for me?

掉頭子 TIAO³ TOU² DZ³, *lit.*, change-header, or 'change-ender', the man who carries at the extreme front of a three or four man chair. 請 TSIN³, please; quite properly used to one's chair-bearer, in asking him to do some unusual service. 給我 GE¹ NGO³, for me, to me; 花生 HWA¹ SEN¹, peanuts; the large peanuts are 大花生 DA⁴ HWA¹ SEN¹. 十個錢的 SHI² GO⁴ TSIEN² DY², ten cash worth; the whole phrase modifies 花生 HWA¹ SEN¹

勞爲你，抬起走

396 Thank you; travel on.

勞爲 LAO² WEI⁴, thanks, thank you; used for service rendered, never in acknowledgment of a gift, for which 道謝 DAO⁴ SIE⁴, or 多謝 DO¹ SIE⁴ is the proper word. This is an important point to remember. Probably no real meaning can be taken from these two characters, they are rather borrowed to express the sounds and tones. It may have been originally 難爲 LAN² WEI², which approaches in meaning the common phrase 作難 DZO² LAN², to obstruct, to make it difficult for.

攏塲我要打尖

397 When we reach the village I want to take a lunch.

攏 LUNG³, to arrive; 塲 CHANG², village, market; 'when' understood. 要 YAO⁴, I shall, I will, I want, I am about to. 打尖 DA³ GIEN¹, to strike a wedge! To take an interim lunch. Very common, both phrase and act.

要找一個乾淨亮騷的店子

398 I want you to look for a clean light inn.

要找 YAO⁴ DJAO³, want look for; the order is to the man or men addressed, presumably the chairmen. 乾淨 GAN¹ DZIN⁴, clean; 亮騷 LIANG⁴ SAO⁴, light; 店子 DIEN⁴ DZ³, inn. This is better than to request that a *good* inn be found, because Chinese ideas as to what constitutes a good inn probably differ from ours.

要抬進去,不在街上提

399 I want you to carry me in, not put me down on the street.

抬進去 TAI² DZIN⁴ CHÜ⁴, carry enter go, carry into the inn. This is only ordinary politeness to the traveller. If the chair-bearers suspect that the foreigner does not know the difference, they will prefer to place the chair on the street, thereby avoiding the work of carrying into and out of the inn. Ladies should insist on always being carried into the inn, whether for rest or for lunch, unless the place is a very small hamlet, and the day a non-market day.

ON THE ROAD

把伙食挑子擔過來

400 Bring the food load over (here).

王長興、快點把棹子擺起

401 Wang Chang-Hsin, hurry up with the setting of the table.

快點 KWAI⁴ DIEN³, quickly, a little more quickly; 擺起 BAI³ CHI³, to set, as a table.

把茶泡起

402 Make the tea. Or, 'Steep the tea'.

茶 CHA², tea; 泡 PAO⁴, to steep, to soak.

煎兩個蛋

403 Fry two eggs.

煎 DZIEN¹, to fry.

先喊么師傅倒水來洗臉

404 First call the waiter to bring water for face washing.

么師傅 YAO¹ SI¹ FU⁴, the general name for the individual who waits on guests, whether in inns or restaurants. 倒水來 DAO⁴ SHUI³ LAI², empty water come, *i.e.* pour water into a basin and bring it. 洗臉 SI³ LIEN³, to wash face.

155

東西擺歸一沒有

405 Have you put things all out on the table?

擺歸一了

406 Everything is spread.

先生吃不吃米飯

407 Will you have some rice? (Asked by one's own servant, or by the inn waiter).

米 MI³, hulled uncooked rice. 飯 FAN⁴, cooked rice, but its meaning is extended to food generally. Therefore the correct translation is 'rice food'.

可以添個半碗米飯來

408 You may bring me a half bowl of rice.

添 TIEN¹, to add; this is the appropriate word to use in asking for rice in inn or restaurant. 半 BAN⁴, half; 碗 WAN³, bowl; but this expression, 'half bowl' usually means half of a heaping bowl, and therefore about one level bowl of rice.

這一下子吃完了

409 Now I have finished.

完了 WAN² LIAO³, finished; 煞角 SHA² GO², or 煞角了 SHA² GO² LIAO³, same meaning; very much used.

趕緊把東西洗過

410 Hurry with the washing of things.

趕緊 GAN³ GIN³, hurry! *Lit.*, 'Take things (and cause them to be) washed'.

ON THE ROAD

撿在箱子頭

411 Put them away in the boxes.

跟倒趂起來

412 Then quickly catch up with us.

跟倒 GEN¹ DAO³, has two common meanings (1) to follow, and (2) at once, immediately, quickly. Either would be admissable here, but the latter sense is better. 趂 NIEN³, to chase, to catch up with.

不到黑、歇得攏籍田鋪嗎

413 Can we reach Dzi Tien Pu before dark?

不到黑 BU² DAO⁴ HE², not arrive at dark, before dark; 歇 HSIE², to rest, to stay over night; 攏 LUNG³, to arrive. 歇得攏 HSIE² DE² LUNG³, is a curious idiom, best explained, perhaps, by this literal translation, 'Can (we) arrive (in order to) stay over night?' The 嗎 MA¹ indicates the interrogative. 籍田鋪 DZI² TIEN² PU⁴ is the half way village between Chengtu and Jenshow.

不怕得、歇得攏

414 Don't be afraid, we can arrive (before dark).

不怕得 BU² PA⁴ DE², not fear can, do not fear; logically it should be 不怕的 BU² PA⁴ DY², but the common colloquial uses 得 DE¹ mostly. I believe it to be a corruption, certainly; it has probably come into use more because it is a sound more easily emphasized than 的 DY².

攏場、還有好多里

415 How many *li* is it still to the village?

攏場 LUNG³ CHANG², arrive village, *i.e.* in order to arrive at the village ahead. This sentence may be used anywhere on the road, as an enquiry for the distance to the village next ahead, without knowing at all the name of it. 還 HAI², still; 有 YIU³, there is; 好多 HAO³ DO¹, how many; 里 LI³, the Chinese mile, of which there are approximately three and a third to the English mile. But the length of the *li* is only approximate, varying in different parts of the country.

還有十幾里

416 There are still more than ten *li*.

場上有好店子沒得

417 Is there a good inn in the village?

場上 CHANG² SHANG⁴, in the village; like 街上 GAI¹ SHANG⁴, on the street.

有、仁義店有上官房

418 There is; the Benevolence-Righteousness Inn has an upper official room.

This to the average Chinese expresses the difference between an ordinary low-class inn and a *good* inn, "it has an upper official room". In many cases we prefer to place our cots outside said upper official room, in order to get better air and less dust!

總要一個亮騷通風的房圈、纔好

419 I must have a light airy room.

ON THE ROAD

總 DZUNG³, emphatic particle; 通風 TUNG¹ FUNG¹, permeate wind, *i.e.* well-ventilated, airy; 房圓 FANG² CHUEN¹, room, especially a bedroom.

王長興、可以朝前頭跑去打店

420 Wang Chang-Hsin, you may run on ahead, (in order to) secure the inn.

朝 CHAO², towards; 前頭 TSIEN² TOU², in front, ahead; 跑 PAO³, to run; 打店 DA³ DIEN⁴, *lit.*, strike the inn; secure room or rooms in the inn.

攏了店、下了轎子

421 We have arrived at the inn and got out of our chairs.

下 HSIA⁴, to descend from; commonly used for getting out of one's chair; 出來 CHU² LAI², come out, is also used for the same act.

挑子也攏齊了

422 The loads have also all arrived.

齊 TSI², all, together, complete; very common.

挑子不忙一下

423 You load coolies, don't be in a hurry for a minute.

Lit., Loads! Not hurry a little. That is to say, don't be in a hurry to place the loads for the night. 不忙 BU² MANG², don't be in such a hurry; often has 多 DO¹ added,—不忙多 BU² MANG² DO¹, same meaning; the character 多 DO¹ is quite meaningless here.

先看一下房圈

424 I want to look at the rooms first.

好、我歇這一間

425 Good! I shall occupy this one.

歇 HSIE[2], to stay over night in; 間 GIEN[1], classifier for room.

把挑子擔進來

426 Bring the loads in.

擔進來 DAN[1] DZIN[4] LAI[2], carry enter come, bring in.

把箱子排好

427 Arrange the boxes properly.

排 PAI[2], to place in order, to arrange in a row. HAO[3], orderly, in a convenient way.

鎖向外頭、好打開

428 (Place them with) the locks towards the outside, for convenience in opening.

鎖 SO[3], locks; 向 HSIANG[4], towards; 外頭 WAI[4] TOU[2], outside; 好 HAO[3], for convenience in; 打開 DA[3] KAI[1], to open, as a box, a door; *lit.*, to strike open.

索子都要解開

429 (I want) all the ropes untied.

解開 GAI[3] KAI[1], to untie, to loosen.

ON THE ROAD

扁擔斗笠放在這裡不
怕得

430 Put your carrying poles and rain hats here, no fear.

扁擔 BIEN³ DAN⁴, 'flat load', carrying poles, which are flattened in shape. 斗笠 DOU³ LI², rain hats, the big wide-brimmed hats made of bamboo, well woven so as to shed the rain, and in a measure also to shelter from the hot sun.

王長興可以把我的床
攔在這外前

431 Wang Chang-Hsin, you may make up my bed outside here.

攔 BA⁴, to make up a bed, to place a bed; see 386. The character 前 TSIEN² at the end of this sentence is almost certain to be pronounced in the first tone, for euphony's sake.

把罩子掛起

432 Hang up (my) mosquito net.

罩子 DJAO⁴ DZ³, net, a lamp-globe; 掛起 GWA⁴ CHI³, hang up.

把棹子擺起

433 Set the table.

把這一盒菜拿去熱滾

434 Take this tin of vegetables and heat it to boiling.

盒 HO², a small tin or box, whose lid lifts off, 熱 RE², to heat; used here as a verb. 滾 GWEN³, to boil, to bubble as boiling water.

號錢、今晚上要給清

435 The inn money you must pay to-night.

號錢 HAO⁴ TSIEN², *lit.*, registration money, inn charges; 今晚上 GIN¹ WAN³ SHANG⁴, this evening; 清 TSIN¹, clear, *i.e.* in their entirety.

拿好多號錢、先生

436 How much inn money shall I pay?

給他兩個說、就是咯

437 Argue prices with him, that's the only thing to do.

給 GE¹, here 'with'; 兩個 LIANG³ GO⁴, two; 說 SHO², here 'argue', discuss'. 給他兩個 GE¹ TA¹ LIANG³ GO⁴, with him the two of you .... a beautiful idiom, clear and expressive. Inns have no fixed charges.

總是每乘轎子、一百幾兩百錢

438 Of course it will be one hundred odd to two hundred cash per chair.

每乘轎子 MEI³ CHEN² GIAO⁴ DZ³, each chair. The 'to' after 'odd' is not needed at all in Chinese.

明早上、給么師傅幾十個錢茶錢

439 To-morrow morning give the waiter several tens of cash as tea money.

ON THE ROAD

明早上 MIN² DZAO³ SHANG⁴, to-morrow morning; 茶錢 CHA² TSIEN², tea-money, tip.

可以給他們夫子說, 明天走得早

440 You may tell the coolies that we shall start early to-morrow.

夫子 FU¹ DZ³, coolies, *i.e.* 轎夫 GIAO⁴ FU¹, chair coolies, and 挑夫 TIAO¹ FU¹, load coolies. 早 DZAO³, early. For the construction 他們夫子 TA¹ MEN² FU¹ DZ³, see 371.

天未亮, 我們起來收拾東西

441 Before daylight we shall get up and put things into shape.

未 WEI⁴, not yet; 起來 CHI³ LAI², to get up;

天亮咯, 天亮咯, 起來了

442 Daylight, daylight! Get up!

The addition of the 咯 LO² after 天亮 TIEN¹ LIANG⁴, implies that it is not merely about to get light, it is already light. The use of the 了 LIAO³ with 起來 CHI³ LAI² greatly softens the call, whether to one's own servants or to the chair and load coolies.

還早得很先生

443 It is still very early!

This is heard in a sleepy voice from the depths of a windowless room, and much persistence may be required on our part to convince the owner of his error.

王長興，把夫頭喊起來

444　Wang Chang-Hsin, call the head coolie.

夫頭 FU[1] TOU[2], the head man with whom we do all our negotiating on the road; 喊起來 HAN[3] CHI[3] LAI[2], call get up, call him up; this is a peremptory order, much stronger than the 起來了 CHI[3] LAI[2] LIAO[3] above. FU[1] TOU[2] is often corrupted to FU[1] TER[2].

來了，來了

445　Coming, coming!

This is the head man's answer, as he emerges from his bedroom, drawing on his clothes as he comes.

挑子裝歸一了

446　The loads are all packed and ready.

可以擔起走

447　Make a start with them.

走好遠吃飯

448　How far shall we go before breakfast?

遠 YUEN[3], far, distant; 好遠 HAO[3] YUEN[3], how far?

ON THE ROAD

走二十里吃早飯

449 We shall go twenty *li* and have breakfast.

今天落雨、路爛又溜

450 It is raining to-day; the roads are muddy and slippery.

落雨 LO² YÜ³, it is raining; 路爛 LU⁴ LAN⁴, the roads are muddy; 又溜 YIU⁴ LIU¹, also slippery. 滑 HWA² is another common word meaning 'slippery'; both much used.

今天走得攏嗎、走不攏

451 Can we get there to-day or not?

走得攏 DZOU³ DE² LUNG³, travel can arrive = we can get there; 走不攏 DZOU³ BU² LUNG³, travel not arrive = we cannot get there.

今天橫順要走攏、先生

452 We are determined to arrive to-day.

橫順 HWAN² SHWEN⁴, 'crosswise-lengthwise', *i.e.* under any circumstances. The character 橫 is adapted for this word. It is also pronounced HWEN².

王長興、你要長行同挑子一路

453 Wang Chang-Hsin, you must keep constantly with the loads.

長行 CHANG² HSIN², always; this is the commonest Chinese word for 'always'. 同 TUNG²..... 一路 I² LU⁴, with.... one road, *i.e.* together with.

催他們快點走

454 Urge them to travel a little faster.

催 TSUI¹, to urge.

你們轎子上的，放不放加班

455 Will you chair-bearers let out your jobs or not?

轎子上的 GIAO⁴ DZ³ SHANG⁴ DY², on-the-chairs-men, the character 人 REN², being understood. 加班 GIA¹ BAN¹, bearers who are hired by the regular men to carry in their places for short distances *en route*. 放加班 FANG⁴ GIA¹ BAN¹, to let out one's work to these extra men. GIA¹ BAN¹ is often corrupted to GIA¹ BER¹.

亮葉子說，我不放

456 The light-leaf said, 'I will not let out my job',

LIANG⁴ YE² DZ³, light-leaf, literally; this is the second man from the front, on either a three-man or a four-man chair. Why so called is not well understood; I have heard various explanations, mostly far-fetched. On a four-man chair, the third man from the front is called 黑窩子 HE² WO¹ DZ³, dark nest. This man is well named, for he cannot see anything except just at his feet.

我那頭放過咯

457 I let out my job back yonder.

This is a continuation of the remark by light-leaf. 那頭 LA⁴ TOU², at that end, *i.e.* back behind somewhere. 過咯 GO⁴ LO², both signs of the past tense.

ON THE ROAD

那個加班搬不來杵

458 That extra bearer is not capable of handling the upright.

搬 BAN¹, to move [move written above "manage" crossed out]; 搬不來 BAN¹ BU² LAI², incapable of moving [written above "managing" crossed out]; 杵 CHU³, the upright which is used to support the weight of the chair while changing shoulders.

後欄子說,說得合式我要放

459 The rear man said, 'If we can agree on a satisfactory rate I will let out my job'.

後欄子 HOU⁴ BA⁴ DZ³, the rear man. This is the name given to the last man on either three- or four-bearer chairs. 合式 HO² SHI⁴, agreeable, satisfactory; 說得合式 SHO² DE² HO² SHI⁴, to talk secure satisfactory, *i.e.* come to an agreement.

果然不到黑就攏了

460 We really did arrive before dark.

果然 GO³ RAN², really, certainly.

挑子也齊了

461 The loads also are all here.

齊 TSI², together, all together.

可以喊夫頭進來

462 You may call the head coolie in.

要清下脚給他

463 I want to pay him the balance due.

清 TSIN¹, *lit.*, clear, clearly; here 'to clear', 'to reckon clearly'. 下 脚 HSIA⁴ GIO², *lit.*, lower foot, *i.e.* remainder; 給 他 GE¹ TA¹, give him, pay to him.

請先生給點茶錢

464 Please give a little tea money.

茶 錢 CHA² TSIEN², tea money, "cumshaw", tips.

王長興,可以數五十個錢一個人給他們

465 Wang Chang-Hsin, you may count out fifty cash for each man and give to them.

數 SU³, to count; 數 給 SU³ GE¹, count give, *i.e.* pay over to. 一 個 人 I² GO⁴ REN², one man, *i.e.* each man.

LESSON 15. 第十五課

換銀元

Changing Dollars

換銀元

466   Changing dollars.

  銀元 YIN² YUEN², silver coin, the dollar, any subsidiary coin, as the ten-, twenty- or fifty-cent piece. But the dollar is gradually coming to be meant by the straight term 'yin yuen'. The term 洋錢 YANG² TSIEN², used so much at the coast, is rarely heard in West China.

王長興,今天銀元換甚麼價

467   Wang Chang-Hsin, what does the dollar change for to-day?

  Note that the time or date comes first, not last as in English.

今天換得倒一吊五百五的樣子

468   It changes to-day for about 1550 cash.

  換得倒 HWAN⁴ DE² DAO³, can be changed for as much as; 一吊 I² DIAO⁴, one string, *i.e.* one thousand cash; 樣子 YANG⁴ DZ³, sort, fashion; *i.e.* 'about', thereabouts'.

是不是盡銅元

469 Does that mean wholly for coppers?

盡 DZIN⁴, wholly, completely; 銅元 TUNG² YUEN², copper coins, as opposed to the old style cash with the square holes through them.

是盡銅元

470 Yes, that is for coppers only.

有底子沒得

471 Is there any deficiency?

底子 DI³ DZ³, the regular "deficiency" accepted and acknowledged by the custom of the place. One city may have the custom of regarding 990 cash as a string; another 980, or 986, as the case may be; while still other places, as Chengtu for instance, always give full 1000 cash to the string. The 底子 DI³ DZ³ is therefore the amount less than 1000 accepted by custom.

足錢沒得底

472 Full-count cash, no deficiency.

足 DZU², enough, full. This character is also written instead of 脚 GIO², and is then better pronounced GIO².

有些地方銅元少,小錢多

473 In some places the coppers are scarce, but the "small cash" is plentiful.

CHANGING DOLLARS

"In" is understood at the beginning of the sentence. 有些 YIU³ SIE¹, some; 地方 DI⁴ FANG¹, place, places; 小錢 SIAO³ TSIEN², lit., small cash, i.e. the old style cash with the square hole.

換小錢定有底、一吊錢十個、或十幾個

474 If you change for small cash, there will certainly be a deficiency, ten or ten odd cash to the thousand.

定 DIN⁴, certainly, surely; 有底 YIU³ DI³, there is or there will be a deficiency; 或 HWE², or, perhaps.

多半又有少數、一二十個

475 Probably there will also be a short count of ten to to twenty.

多半 DO¹ BAN⁴, 'more half', i.e. probably; 少數 SHAO³ SU⁴, less count, i.e. 'short count' something quite different from the 底子 DI³ DZ³. The short count is not acknowledged by custom; it is always an attempt at fraud, and the amount is usually cheerfully made up by the cash shop proprietor if discovered in time. The latter trusts to lack of time and patience on the part of his customer for counting the long strings of thousands of small cash; and his confidence is usually well placed, when he is dealing with foreigners. Hence the advantage of using the new copper coins, which can be counted so quickly and accurately.

肯換盡銅元

476 I prefer to exchange for coppers only.

肯 KEN³, to be willing, to prefer; 盡 DZIN⁴, wholly; here readily translated by 'only'.

可以把這五塊錢拿去，換了來

477 You may take these five dollars and change them.

五塊錢 WU³ KWAI³ TSIEN², five dollars; 一塊錢 I² KWAI³ TSIEN², one dollar, very commonly used instead of 一圓 I² YUEN². 拿去換了來 LA² CHŪ⁴ HWAN⁴ LIAO³ LAI², "take away exchanged come"; very clear and free from ambiguity.

拿回來，要數清楚

478 When you have brought the cash back, you are to count it carefully.

'When' understood; the word 'cash' is not mentioned, but it is clear from what has gone before that this is what is being talked about; there can be nothing else. Therefore it is unnecessary to express the word—this is the usual Chinese argument.

一吊一吊的包起

479 The cash is then to be wrapped up, a thousand in a package.

一吊一吊的 I² DIAO⁴ I² DIAO⁴ DY², thousand by thousand; compare 一個一個的 I² GO⁴ I² GO⁴ DY², one by one. The 的 DY² in these phrases most often flies up into the first tone. 包 BAO¹, to wrap up; 起 CHI³, is added in order to complete the sense, and to make a dissyllable.

LESSON 16. 第十六課

換銀子

Changing Silver

換銀子

480 Changing Silver.

銀子 YIN², DZ³, silver, *i.e.* lump silver or sycee, which was the only kind of silver money known in West China up to 1898.

王長興，今天銀子甚麼過頭

481 Wang Chang-Hsin, what is the rate of exchange for silver to-day?

Note again that the time, 'to-day', is expressed immediately after the name, and at the beginning of the question. Note also the absence of any verb. 過頭 GO⁴ TOU², rate of exchange; also 行市 HANG² SHI⁴, both much used.

多久沒有換過，不曉得

482 For a long time I have not changed any; I do not know.

多久 DO¹ GIU³, much long time, *i.e.* 'for a long time'; 過 GO⁴, sign of past tense.

可以去問一下

483　You may go and ask.

問一下 WEN⁴ I² HA⁴, 'ask a little'; the 一下 I² HA⁴ softens the command.

要多問幾處、纔要得

484　You must ask at several places, in order to be sure.

幾處 GI³ CHU⁴, several places; 多問 DO¹ WEN⁴, 'more ask', a very common idiom that seems scarcely capable of a logical explanation. The effect of the whole phrase 多問幾處 DO¹ WEN⁴ GI³ CHU⁴, seems to be, 'Ask in quite a large number of places'. 要得 YAO⁴ DE², satisfactory. satisfactory.

他回來的時候說

485　When he came back he said,

This is the first part of the sentence, continued in 486.

銀子今天換得倒二十二吊的光景

486　Silver can be changed to-day at about twenty-two thousand cash.

的光景 DY² GWANG¹ GIN³, about; a common idiom; the phrase is placed usually at the end of the sentence, as here. The word 錢 TSIEN², cash, is understood after 吊 DIAO⁴.

CHANGING SILVER

有一家只出二十一吊七

487 One shop would pay only twenty-one thousand seven hundred.

有一家 YIU³ I² GIA¹, there was one family; here 'one firm' or 'one shop'; 只 GI³, only; 出 CHU², to come out, to go out; here 'to pay out'.

又有一家出二十一吊八

488 There was another firm that offered twenty-one thousand eight hundred.

These prices are per ten tæls, or ounces of silver, of course. Note the ending of the sentence with 八 BA², eight; 'hundred' is understood after it, in both this sentence and the one above.

有一個米粮舖答應了二十二吊錢

489 There was a provision shop that agreed to twenty-two thousand cash.

米 MI³, rice; 粮 LIANG², provisions; 舖 PU⁴, shop; 答應 DA² YIN⁴, answered, agreed to.

說的是銅元嗎,小錢

490 Was it coppers you agreed on, or small cash?

Lit., 'Talked was coppers or, etc.' 說的 SHO² DY², talked, argued.

小錢、他包沒得少數

491 Small cash; he guarantees that there will be no short-count.

包 BAO¹, to guarantee, to wrap up; 少數 SHAO³ SU⁴, short-count or shortage, not technical "deficiency" allowed by custom.

有十六個底

492 There would be sixteen cash deficiency.

Note the idiom by which the 子 DZ³ is dropped at the end; I don't know why, except that it may be for brevity.

先生換好多銀子

493 How much silver do you wish to change?

That is to say, how many tæls? A tæl is an ounce.

我只換一錠

494 I wish to change a ten-tæl piece only.

錠 DÍN⁴, a ten-tæl lump, which weighs anywhere from nine to eleven tæls. It is never calculated to make these "ten tæl lumps" weigh exactly ten tæls. Each lump has to be weighed at least once by every individual who handles it.

這一錠、重九兩六錢八

495 This lump weighs nine tæls and sixty-eight cents.

Note the absence of any verb. It is not required by Chinese idiom.

CHANGING SILVER

你可以請一個人幫忙拷回來

496 You may hire a man to help you carry the cash back.

請 TSIN³, here 'to hire'; 幫忙 BANG¹ MANG², to help, in the commonest sense; very much used; 拷 LAO³, to carry on the shoulder, as one does a hoe or other similar utensil; 回來 HWEI² LAI², to return, to come home. One string of the old-fashioned small cash weighs ten or twelve pounds.

錢拷回來了

497 The cash has been brought home.

王長興、這個錢不對

498 Wang Chang-Hsin, this cash is not right.

這個錢 DJE⁴ GO⁴ TSIEN², lit., this one cash, but here used in the sense of 'this cash'; 不對 BU² DUI⁴, not correct, not right, will not do.

毛錢多得很

499 The spurious cash is very numerous.

毛錢 MAO² TSIEN², spurious cash, the very thin, rough, small cash introduced among the good cash exactly as any adulterant is introduced into any otherwise good article of commerce. The effect is, of course, to reduce the value of the whole; but this gives numberless opportunities for argument and haggling, with the possibility of slightly increased profit to some one,—and corresponding loss to another.

他說使不脫的包換

500 He said that he would guarantee to change any that proved unusable.

This forms the plausible argument of the smooth-talking cash-shop dealer. 使不脫的 SHĬ³ BU² TO² DY², with 錢 TSIEN² understood at the end, *lit.*, 'use not part from'; *i.e.* unable-to-get-rid-of cash; 包換 BAO¹ HWAN⁴, guarantee exchange. Again he trusts to the lack of time or of patience or of both, in his customers.

要不得

501 That is very bad; or, That will not do.

A very common and very strong phrase. Food may not be very tasty, yet eatable, and we might say it is 不大好 BU² DA⁴ HAO³; if it were still less pleasant, almost unusable, we might call it bad, 不好 BU² HAO³; if it is spoiled and quite unusable, we say it is 要不得 YAO⁴ BU² DE², very bad, and must be thrown out. This series of phrases may be applied to conduct in a very similar way.

你曉得我們沒有用毛錢

502 You know we are not in the habit of using spurious cash.

沒有用毛錢 MU² YIU³ YUNG⁴ MAO² TSIEN², logically should be 'have not used spurious cash'; but here it has the force of the translation given.

爲啥子換這麼多毛錢來

503 Why have you accepted (in exchange) so much spurious cash?

CHANGING SILVER

Lit., Why exchanged so much spurious cash come? 為啥子 WEI⁴ SHA⁴ DZ³, common colloquial for 為甚麼 WEI⁴ SHEN⁴ MO³, why. 這麼多 DJE⁴ MO³ DO¹, thus much, this much.

把連一下耍捞轉去掉

504 You may take the whole lot back and exchange it.

把連一下 BA³ LIEN² I² HA⁴, all, the whole lot; 捞轉去 LAO³ DJWAN³ CHÜ⁴, carry back on your shoulders; 掉 TIAO³, to change, to exchange; constantly interchanged with 換 HWAN⁴.

第二次捞錢回來了

505 The cash has been carried home the second time.

第二次 DI⁴ ER⁴ TSI⁴, the second time; also 第二回 DI⁴ ER⁴ HWEI², same meaning. Both very common.

王長興可以把這一吊錢拿來數過

506 Wang Chang-Hsin, you may take this string of cash and count it.

一吊錢 I² DIAO⁴ TSIEN², one string of cash, one thousand cash. What is the force of the 拿來 LA² LAI²? It is just 'bring' or 'bring here', and seems to have some sense of defining or specially denoting this particular one thousand cash. It might be omitted without seriously harming the sentence.

數得好多

507 How many do you count? Or, How many are there?

纔九百七十二個錢

508 There are only nine hundred and seventy-two cash.

纔 TSAI², only, which varies somewhat from its usual meaning of 'then and not till then'. 有 YIU³, there are, understood after 纔 TSAI².

這是怎個的

509 How is this?

A very common colloquial idiom, much used in Chengtu. 怎個的 DZA² GO⁴ DY², how, but this 'how' is expressed with terrific emphasis in this idiom. One might say, 'How in the world?' It may be also translated 'why', as 昨天怎個沒有來 DZO² TIEN¹ DZA² GO⁴ MU² YIU³ LAI², 'Why did you not come yesterday?' This is the character DZEN³ in the phrase 怎麼樣 DZEN³ MO³ YANG⁴, very common in the scripture, and to a certain degree in speech.

扣了十六個錢的底、還要爭十二個錢

510 After deducting sixteen cash deficiency, there are still twelve cash lacking.

底 DI³, recognized 'deficiency'; 要 YAO⁴, will; seems as thrown in here from force of habit; logically the sentence is better without it. 爭 DZEN¹, lacks, to lack. ~~This character is borrowed for its sound, as indicated by the 日 added to it on the left. There is no proper character for it.~~ These twelve cash are what are ordinarily called 'short count' or 'shortage', which is unrecognized and unregulated, by any custom, and always results from an attempt to defraud.

CHANGING SILVER

還耍拷轉去

511 You must carry it back again.

還 HAI², still, yet, again; often read HWAN², and sometimes so spoken. 拷轉去 LAO³ DJWAN³ CHÜ⁴, carry back.

我跟掌櫃說一下,

512 I shall talk to the proprietor

跟 GEN¹, to; same in this usage exactly as 給 GE¹, perhaps not quite so much used as 給 GE¹. This sentence is spoken by the servant, and finished in 513.

請他補,使得嗎

513 and ask him to make it up; will that do?

That is, he proposes to ask the proprietor to make up the 'shortage', not the 'deficiency'. His fraud is discovered, and he is to be asked to make good; but he will not be chagrined, except at having failed to make that little profit. He can always plausibly explain the matter as the oversight of his clerk! 補 BU³, to mend, to make up a shortage; 使得嗎 SHĪ³ DE² MA¹, will that do? Very common, and usable in all sorts of situations.

還是使得

514 Yes, that will do.

This answer on the part of the master to his servant implies that the course suggested is an alternative to some other possible course. This is shown in the two characters 還是 HAI² SHĪ⁴, still is.

那個說小錢不淘氣

515 Who says that small cash are not annoying!

那個 LA³ GO⁴, who; 淘氣 TAO² CHI⁴, annoying, irritating. Very common.

LESSON 17. 第十七課

擦 燈

Cleaning the Lamp

擦 燈

516 Cleaning the lamp.

擦 TSA², to rub; 燈 DEN¹, a lamp, lamps.

趙興順,可以過來一下

517 Djao Hsin-Shwen, come here a minute.

過來一下 GO⁴ LAI² I² HA⁴, 'come here a little', about the pleasantest way of calling a servant to one, especially with the 可以 KO³ I³ prefixed to it.

我要教你擦燈

518 I want to teach you to clean lamps.

教 GIAO¹, to teach; remember the first tone for this word, when used thus in familiar conversation.

先把玻璃罩子,玻璃筒筒,取下來

519 First take off the glass shade and the glass chimney.

玻璃 BO¹ LI², glass, the material; 罩子 DJAO⁴ DZ³, lamp globe or shade; 筒筒 TUNG² TUNG¹, lit., tube, the glass tube, i.e. the glass chimney. The average Chinese coolie will apply the one word 罩子 DJAO⁴ DZ³ to both shade and chimney, resulting in confusion. These are terms that we have to teach them, because lamps are only now being introduced, and they have as yet no fixed terms of their own. 取下來 CHÜ³ HSIA⁴ LAI², to take off, to take down, as a garment or a hat off a nail.

把燈眼蓋蓋車脫

520 Unscrew the cap of the lamp-hole

燈眼 DEN¹ YEN³, lamp hole, the opening through which oil is poured; 蓋蓋 GAI⁴ GAI¹, cap, cover; note change of tone of duplicated character, for the sake of euphony. 車 CHE¹, to turn; 脫 TO², off, to come off.

拿廠子挿進去

521 Bring the funnel and stick it in.

廠子 CHANG³ DZ³, funnel; also sometimes called 漏斗 LOU⁴ DOU³. 挿 CHA², to stick into, as a post into the ground, a flower in a vase, a funnel into an opening.

上滿油

522 Fill it full of oil.

上 SHANG⁴, to fill; 上燈 SHANG⁴ DEN¹, to fill the lamps; 上鐘 SHANG⁴ DJUNG¹, to wind the clock; 上油 SHANG⁴ YIU², to fill with oil. 滿 MAN³, full.

CLEANING THE LAMP

油不要上滿很了

523 Do not fill it too full!

油 YIU², oil, may be omitted in the English translation. 很了 HEN³ LIAO³, too.

又把蓋蓋車上去

524 Now screw the cap on.

車上去 CHE¹ SHANG⁴ CHÜ⁴, screw on go, to screw on.

這一下子、把燈心子車上來

525 Now then turn up the wick.

燈心子 DEN¹ SIN⁴ DZ³, lamp wick; the character 心 SIN⁴ comes about as near as we can get to the meaning we want but the tone has to be changed to fourth, to accord with the way it is spoken. 車上來 CHE¹ SHANG⁴ LAI², turn up come.

用指拇、把燈花拈乾淨、把心子弄齊

526 With your fingers pinch the burnt wick off clean, and make the wick even.

Lit., 'With fingers take burnt wick pinch clean; take wick make even'. 指拇 GI³ MU³, fingers; 燈花 DEN¹ HWA¹, burnt wick, *lit.*, lamp flower; 弄 LUNG¹, to make, to cause to be; 齊 TSI², even, together.

CHINESE LESSONS

不用剪刀剪

527 Do not use the scissors to cut (the wick) off.

剪刀 DZIEN³ DAO¹, scissors; 剪 DZIEN³, to cut with scissors.

爲咪子不用剪刀

528 Why should I not use the scissors?

用剪刀費心子

529 If you use the scissors you will waste the wick.

費 FEI⁴, to waste; 枉費 WANG³ FEI⁴, is the dissyllabic form; a very common word meaning 'to waste' is 遭踏 DZAO¹ TA²; in fact it is much more used than 枉費 WANG³ FEI⁴.

二則，剪不倒那麼勻淨

530 Furthermore, you cannot cut so evenly with the scissors.

二則 ER⁴ DZE², in the second place, furthermore; 剪不倒 DZIEN³ BU² DAO³, cannot cut (with scissors); 勻淨 YUIN² DZIN⁴, evenly, uniformly.

把龍頭擦乾淨

531 Rub the burner clean.

龍頭 LUNG² TOU², the lamp-burner; this is one of two or three names that may be adapted for 'burner' in Chinese; *lit.*, 'dragon-head'.

把燈壺脚脚擦乾净

532 Rub the foot of the lamp clean.

CLEANING THE LAMP 173

Lit., 'the foot of the lamp-bowl'. 壺 FU², bowl of the lamp; it is the 'pot' of teapot, 茶壺 CHA² FU².

用乾淨帕子,把玻璃筒筒擦乾淨

533 With a clean cloth wipe the lamp chimney clean.

乾淨帕子 GAN¹ DZIN⁴ PA⁴ DZ³, clean cloth; 擦 TSA², to rub, to wipe.

裏外吹點氣,就好擦

534 Inside and outside blow your breath, and it will be easy to clean.

裏外 LI³ WAI⁴, inside outside; 吹 CHUI¹, to blow; 氣 CHI⁴, breath; 就好擦 DZIU⁴ HAO³ TSA², then (it will be) good (to) rub, *i.e.* it will be easy to clean.

把燈罩子擦乾淨

535 Rub the shade clean.

把燈筒燈罩安起

536 Put chimney and shade in place (on the lamp).

安起 NGAN¹ CHI³, to put in place.

全燈擦得乾乾净净的

537 The whole lamp is rubbed perfectly clean.

全 CHUEN², the whole, entire; 擦得 TSA² DE², logically 擦的 TSA² DY³, but the former is what seems to be used most. The duplication of the characters in the word meaning 'clean' expresses emphasis; hence 'perfectly clean'.

把燈端去擱在原處

538 Carry the lamp away and put it where it belongs.

端 DWAN¹, to carry, with arms extended in front as one carries a lamp; 擱在原處 KO⁴ DZAI⁴ YUEN² CHU⁴, put in original place, i.e. 'where it belongs'.

回回要把細得很

539 You must be very careful every time

把細 BA³ SI⁴, careful; 得很 DE² HEN³, very, extremely.

不要把玻璃打爛

540 lest you break the glass.

This is really the continuation of 539, although worded as though it were an independent sentence. It is literally, 'Don't break the glass'. 打爛 DA³ LAN⁴, to strike broken, to break.

常用的燈天天都要擦

541 The lamps in constant use are to be cleaned every day.

常用的燈 SHANG² YUNG⁴ DY² DEN¹, lit., the constantly-used lamps. 擦 TSA², rubbed, i.e. cleaned.

或者隔一天上油都使得

542 Perhaps if they are filled with oil every other day, that will do.

CLEANING THE LAMP 175

或者 HWE² DJE³, perhaps; which is rather a better word for 'perhaps' than 恐怕 KUNG³ PA¹. The Chinese do not make use of any word meaning 'perhaps' so much as we do. 隔一天 GE² I² TIEN¹, separate one day, *i.e.* every other day; 上油 SHANG⁴ YIU², to fill with oil; 都使得 DU¹ SHÏ³ DE², that will do, that will answer the purpose.

LESSON 18. 第十八課

洗 碗

Washing Dishes

洗碗

543　Washing dishes.

　　碗 WAN³, a bowl, bowls; here expanded to the more general meaning of 'dishes'.

王長興,把碗收完了沒有

544　Wang Chang-Hsin, have you cleared away all the dishes?

　　收 SHOU¹, to receive, to clear away; 完了 WAN² LIAO³, finished.

收完了

545　I have cleared them all away.

先要裝在洗碗盆子頭

546　You must first put them into the dish-basin.

　　裝 DJWANG¹, to put into, see 354. 洗碗盆子 SI³ WAN³ PEN² DZ³, wash bowl basin, *i.e.* 'dish-basin'. 在頭 DZAI⁴ TOU², with 裏 LI³ understood between, = inside.

190

WASHING DISHES

倒開水在高頭

547 Pour boiling water on them.

倒 DAO⁴, to empty; 開水 KAI¹ SHUI³, boiling water; 在高頭 DZAI⁴ GAO¹ TOU², on the top of; also 在上頭 DZAI⁴ SHANG⁴ TOU², same meaning.

用洗碗帕子,一個一個的洗

548 With the dish-cloth wash them one by one.

洗碗帕子 SI³ WAN³ PA⁴ DZ³, wash bowl cloth, *i.e.* dish-cloth.

水燙,就好洗乾淨

549 If your water is hot, it will be easy to wash them clean.

燙 TANG⁴, to scald, to burn by means of hot water or any hot article. 'If' is understood.

把碗燙過,又好撋光生

550 If you scald your dishes, you will also be able to polish them easily.

撋光生 MA² GWANG¹ SEN¹, to wipe smooth, *i.e.* to polish.

洗出來了,就用撋碗帕撋乾

551 When you have washed them, use the tea-towel to wipe them dry.

'When' is understood. 洗出來了 SI³ CHU² LAI² LIAO³, washed come out, *i.e.* when they have passed through the washing stage. 用 YUNG⁴, to use; 搣碗帕 MA² WAN³ PA⁴, wipe dish cloth, *i.e.* the tea-towel; 搣乾 MA² GAN¹, to wipe dry.

盤子一個一個的搣

552 Wipe the plates one by one.

盤子 PAN² DZ³, plates. Sometimes this word, plates, is used as a general name for 'dishes' instead of bowl. Either will do.

不可兩個兩個的搣

553 You must not wipe them two at a time;

不可 BU² KO³, you must not; 兩個兩個的 LIANG³ GO⁴ LIANG³ GO⁴ DY², two two, *i.e.* two at a time.

帕掉下來打爛

554 I fear you will drop them and break them.

怕 PA⁴, (I) fear; 掉下來 DIAO⁴ HSIA⁴ LAI², drop down come, *i.e.* drop to the floor; 打爛 DA³ LAN⁴, to break.

盤子要搣來發光

555 The plates are to be wiped until they shine.

光 GWANG¹, light. 搣來 MA² LAI², somewhat similar to 拿來 LA² LAI² in 506; the LAI² here helps the MA² to get away from the monosyllable. Note how so many of these sentences begin with the noun, the most important word in the sentence.

WASHING DISHES

花的耍不得

556 It will not do to have them streaked.

花的 HWA¹ DY¹, lit., flowered; here 'streaked', see 169.

抹完了，就撿在櫃子頭

557 When the dishes are all wiped, you may put them away in the cupboard.

的時候 DY² SHI² HOU⁴, when, is understood after 了 LIAO³; 撿 GIEN³, to put away; 櫃子 GWEI⁴ DZ³, cupboard, see 188.

刀义調羹，各撿各處

558 Knives, forks and spoons, each (sort) is to be put away in its own place.

刀 DAO¹, knives; often with a DZ³, 刀子 DAO¹ DZ³; 义 CHA¹, or 义子 CHA¹ DZ³, forks; 調羹 TIAO² GEN¹, spoons. 各撿各處 GO² GIEN³ GO² CHU², lit., 'each put away each place'.

抹碗帕，萬不可拿來抹甚麼髒東西

559 Tea towels must not under any circumstances be used to wipe any dirty thing.

萬 WAN⁴, here an emphatic particle; 甚麼 SHEN⁴ MO³, any, when not interrogative; if interrogative, 'what'. 髒 DZANG¹, dirty.

稍微有一点髒，就耍拿去洗

560 If (an article) is the least bit dirty, then it must be taken away and washed.

稍微 SHAO¹ WEI², a very little; 有一点髒 YIU³ I² DIEN³ DZANG¹, there is a little dirt, or 'a little dirty'; 拿去洗 LA² CHÜ⁴ SI³, take away and wash it.

搣碗帕用過,就眼起

561 When you have finished using a tea towel, you must hang it up.

用過 YUNG⁴ GO⁴, used, *i.e.* have finished using; 眼起 LANG⁴ CHI³, or 晾起 LIANG⁴ CHI³, to hang up to dry.

把洗碗帕洗乾淨眼起

562 Wash the dish-cloth clean and hang it up to dry.

把洗碗水倒了

563 Empty your dish-water.

把洗碗盆,洗乾淨掛起

564 Wash the dish-pan clean and hang it up.

Note that the dish-basin is 'hung up', not 'hung up to dry' like the cloths.

LESSON 19. 第十九課

厨房

The Kitchen

厨房

565 The kitchen.

    厨房 CHU² FANG² is a rather more polished term than 竈房 DZAO⁴ FANG², but either is usable.

王長興, 我給你說個話

566 Wang Chang Hsin, I want to speak a word to you:

我們這個厨房常常要乾淨

567 This kitchen of ours must always be kept clean.

    我們這個厨房 NGO³ MEN² DJE⁴ GO⁴ CHU² FANG², we this kitchen, *i.e.* this kitchen of ours. 常常 SHANG² SHANG², the book word for 'always', but quite usable, although 長行 CHANG² HSIN² is more frequently heard. Note that the verb 'kept' is not expressed in Chinese.

地陣, 天天都要洗

568 The floor is to be washed every day.

打雜的可以洗地陣

569　The coolie may wash the floor.

光是要你擔嫌

570　But I want you to bear the responsibility.

　　光是 GWANG¹ SHI⁴ only is, *i.e.* 'only that' or 'but'; 擔 DAN¹, to carry a load with the shoulder-pole, therefore 'to bear'; 嫌 HSIEN², dislike, hate, suspicion; hence 'responsibility'.

灶給家具,你一個人經佑

571　For the cook stove and utensils you must be solely responsible.

　　灶 DZAO⁴, cook-stove; 家具 GIA¹ GŬ¹, utensils; 具 GŬ¹ is read in the fourth tone, but constantly spoken in the first, as here marked. 你一個人 NI³ I² GO⁴ REN², you one man, *i.e.* you alone, you solely; 經佑 GIN¹ YIU¹, to look after, to take care of; very common.

家具常常要乾淨

572　The utensils must be always kept clean.
　　See 567.

或掛在壁頭上

573　They may be either hung on the wall,

或撿在櫃子頭

574　or put away in the cupboard;

THE KITCHEN

或在格格上呬倒

575 they may be placed upside down on the shelves.

格格 GE² GE², shelves; 呬倒 KOU² DAO³, to place with mouth downwards, *i.e.* upside down. This character 呬 KOU² is a borrowed or adapted one.

或撿在抽屜裏頭

576 or put away in drawers;

抽屜 CHOU¹ TI², a drawer or drawers in a cupboard.

總要常常撿得歸歸一一的

577 but in any case they must be put away very neatly.

The duplication of the characters in the last word, meaning neat or neatly, puts much emphasis into it.

不要邋遢

578 Do not be slovenly!

邋遢 LA² TA², slovenly, usually implying dirtiness as well.

還有個話

579 I have still another word (to say to you):

厨房各樣家具,常常要擠在一定的地方

580 Every kind of kitchen utensil is to be always put away in a definite place.

一定的 I² DIN⁴ DY², definite, fixed; 地方 DI⁴ FANG¹, place. Note how this sentence starts with 'kitchen', the most important general noun in it; then follows up with 'utensil', second noun in importance; and then proceeds to remark about these things.

不可亂擱

581 You must not leave them in confusion.

亂 LWAN⁴, confusion, recklessness. 擱 KO⁴, to place; translated rather freely as 'leave'.

不要天天掉地方

582 You must not change the places (of utensils) daily.

掉 TIAO³, to change, to exchange; read DIAO⁴, to drop, to fall to the ground, to lose.

你聽清楚沒有

583 Do you understand clearly?

聽 TIN¹, to hear, to understand, to hear with the understanding; 清楚 TSIN¹ TSU³, clearly, distinctly.

LESSON 20. 第二十課

擺棹子

Setting the Table

擺棹子

584 Setting the table.

擺 BAI³, to spread, to swing back and forth, as a pendulum.

王長興,十二點鐘了,要擺棹子

585 Wang Chang Hsin, it is twelve oclock; you should set the table.

十二點鐘了 SHĬ² ER⁴ DIEN³ DJUNG¹ LIAO³, it is already twelve oclock; the 了 LIAO³ implies that it is *already* twelve oclock, or that it is *fully* twelve oclock.

今天擺乾淨臺帕

586 (You may) put on a clean tablecloth today.

臺帕 TAI² PA⁴, tablecloth.

又擺乾淨手巾

587 (I want you to) also put on clean serviettes.

手巾 SHOU³ GIN¹, *lit.*, hand cloths, a term used by many foreigners for serviettes, although so far as the Chinese is concerned, it would do equally well for 'handkerchiefs'. It would be an advantage if some such term could be generally agreed upon for 'serviette'.

今天擺五個位子

588　Set five places today.

位子 WEI⁴ DZ³, places, positions.

每位擺兩把刀子,兩把义子

589　(At) each place, put two knives and two forks,

每位 MEI³ WEI⁴, each place, with 'at' understood. 把 BA³, the classifier for knife, fork, etc.

一把小調羹、一把二號調羹、一把大調羹

590　one teaspoon, one dessert spoon and one table spoon.

This is a continuation of 589.

把鹽給胡椒、擺起

591　Put on the salt and pepper.

鹽 YEN², salt; 胡椒 HU² GIAO¹, pepper; the character 胡 HU² is very largely changed to FU² in West China.

SETTING THE TABLE

把麵包盤子擺在左手邊

592 Put the bread plates on the left hand side.

麵包 MIEN⁴ BAO¹, bread; 左手邊 DZO³ SHOU³ BIEN¹, left hand side; this translation has the advantage of being perfectly literal.

把麵包、奶油、擺在中間

593 Put the bread and the butter in the centre.

奶油 LAI³ YIU², butter; *lit.*, milk oil; this is the generally used term; it is a good one, and is much to be preferred to the term 黃油 HWANG² YIU², 'yellow oil' used by some.

把白糖、奶子、擺在師母左手邊

594 Place the sugar and milk on the mistress' left hand.

白糖 BE² TANG², sugar; *lit.*, 'white sugar'; 奶子 LAI³ DZ³, milk; this term is much to be preferred to 牛奶 NIU² LAI³, cow's milk, because it does not seem necessary to emphasize every time the fact that it is *cow's* milk that we are using. 師母 SI¹ mu³, the mistress, Mrs., Madame; *lit.*, 'leader mother'.

把茶杯、茶船子、擺在師母右手邊

595 Place the teacups and saucers at the mistress' right hand.

茶杯 CHA² BEI¹, teacup; 茶船子 CHA² CHWAN² DZ³, saucers; *lit.*, tea boats.

把茶壺墊擺起

596 Put the teapot stand on.

茶壺 CHA² FU², teapot; see 532. 墊 DIEN⁴, here the 'stand' on which to set the teapot; something to *put under* something else; a cushion.

把調羹罐子、擺在師母面前

597 Place the teaspoon holder in front of the mistress.

罐子 GWAN⁴ DZ³, a jug; any dish or utensil the shape of a jug; a saucepan. 面前 MIEN¹ TSIEN², in front of.

把大刀子、大叉子、擺在先生的左右

598 Place the carving knife and fork on the right and left of the master.

大刀子 DA⁴ DAO¹ DZ³, the carving knife; 左右 DZO³ YIU⁴, left right, *i.e.* left and right.

把鋼條擺在先生面前

599 Place the steel before the master.

鋼條 GANG¹ TIAO², steel rod, the steel for sharpening the carving knife.

把玻璃杯子、擺一個在各人的右手邊

600 Place a glass tumbler at each person's right hand.

SETTING THE TABLE

玻璃 BO¹ LI², glass; 杯子 BEI¹ DZ³, cup,—glass cup = tumbler. 一個 I² GO⁴, one; 各人的 GO² REN² DY², each person's.

把椅子安好

601 Place the chairs in proper position.

椅子 I³ DZ³, chairs; 安 NGAN¹, to place, to put in place; 好 HAO³, good, right, proper.

LESSON 21. 第二十一課

擺飯

Putting the Food on the Table

擺飯

602 Putting the food on the table.

要依倒鐘點擺飯

603 You must have the food ready on time.

    依倒 I[1] DAO[3], according to; 鐘點 DJUNG[1] DIEN[3], clock point, *i.e.* the time by the clock, the set time.

將將十二點半鐘,就要請大家吃飯

604 At exactly half past twelve o'clock you are to call everybody to dinner.

    將將 DZIANG[1] DZIANG[1], just exactly; 請 TSIN[3], to invite, to call; 大家 DA[4] GIA[1], everybody, the whole family.

請吃飯的時候,就把大湯擺起

605 When you give the call for dinner, then put on the soup.

PUTTING THE FOOD ON THE TABLE

請吃飯 TSIN³ CHI² FAN¹, come to dinner! 大湯 DA⁴ TANG¹, soup; and so 小湯 SIAO³ TANG¹ is commonly used for 'gravy'. 擺起 BAI³ CHI³, put on (the table).

一盤一盤的端來擺

606 Bring the plates (of soup) one at a time, and put them on.

一盤一盤的 I² PAN² I² PAN² DY¹, one plate at a time; 端來 DWAN¹ LAI², bring, as plates are carried.

把細指拇不要唭在湯裏頭去

607 Be careful! Don't stick your fingers into the soup!

唭 CHI¹, a colloquial word, having just this meaning, 'to stick in', or 'to stick out' as one's tongue. This character is borrowed for sound and tone.

跟倒拿冰水來

608 Bring the cold boiled water immediately afterwards.

跟倒 GEN¹ DAO³, immediately; 冰水 BIN¹ SHUI³, lit., iced water or ice water. It is true that we have no such thing in this part of China, but this is a convenient term used by many to distinguish the drinking water which has been boiled and then cooled. At the same time we may get 'to cool' from 冰 BIN¹, which ordinarily means 'to freeze'; hence we may interpret 冰水 BIN¹ SHUI³ as 'to cool water', or 'cooled water'.

給各人倒一杯冰水

609 Pour out a glass of cold water for each one.

Lit., For each person empty one glass cold water.

王長興, 我給你說個要緊的話

610 Wang Chang Hsin, I have an important word to say to you:

Lit., I tell you important words. 給你說 GE[1] NI[3] SHO[2]. to you say, *i.e.* 'tell you'; 要緊 YAO[4] GIN[3], important.

端玻璃杯子的時候

611 When you carry a tumbler,

端 DWAN[1], to carry, as a glass or a cup, or a lamp. This is a part of 610 and 612.

要端底下半節

612 you should take hold of the lower part;

Here 端 DWAN[1] has the sense of 'take hold of'; 底下 DI[3] HSIA[4], below; 半節 BAN[4] DZIE[2], half length, half portion.

不可端倒口口

613 you must not grasp it near the top.

口口 KOU[3] KOU[3], mouth, lip, *i.e.* near the opening or top.

爲脉子

614 Why?

PUTTING THE FOOD ON THE TABLE

因為耍愛乾淨

615 Because you must pay attention to cleanliness;

因為 YIN¹ WEI⁴, because; 愛 NGAI⁴, to love, to be fond of; 愛乾淨 NGAI⁴ GAN¹ DZIN⁴, *lit.*, 'to be fond of being clean' or 'to be fond of cleanliness'.

因為口口耍進人的嘴

616 (and) because the edge of the tumbler must enter a person's mouth.

口口 KOU³ KOU², mouth, lip, edge of the tumbler; the second character of this phrase 口口 KOU³ KOU² almost always drops into the *second* tone, for euphony's sake. 進 DZIN⁴, to enter; 嘴 DZUI³, lips, mouth, spout of a kettle.

還有一個事耍說一下

617 There is another matter of which I wish to speak:

一個事 I² GO⁴ SI⁴, a matter, an affair; 說 SHO², to speak, to talk, to talk about.

端茶杯的時候

618 When you carry teacups,

萬不可把指拇啊進去

619 you must not under any circumstances stick your fingers into them.

Compare 607.

要端在杯子的外頭

620 You must grasp the outside of the cup.

Lit., Must carry on cup's outside.

人家把大湯吃完了

621 (When) people have eaten their soup,

人家 REN² GIA¹, a person, people; very common.

就把湯盤收了

622 then take away the soup plates.

收了 SHOU¹ LIAO³, to take away; *lit.*, 'taken away'.

跟倒把肉給菜,擺在先生面前

623 Then immediately place the meat and vegetables before the master.

肉 RU², meat; constantly corrupted to ROU⁴, a change of both sound and tone. 菜 TSAI⁴, vegetables.

王長興,我舀一盤

624 Wang Chang Hsin, as I serve the plates,

舀 YAO³, to ladle out, to serve on a plate.

你就端一盤給人家

625 you are to carry them to people.

把細,指拇不要喃進菜裏頭去

626 Be careful! Do not stick your fingers into the vegetables.

PUTTING THE FOOD ON THE TABLE

Compare 607 and 619.

菜吃完了,把盤子收咯

627 (When) the vegetables have been eaten, you are to take away the plates.

把點心端來

628 Bring in the dessert.

點心 DIEN³ SIN¹, dessert, confectionery.

又一盤一盤的端給人家

629 Again you are to carry it to people plate by plate.

點心吃完了,把盤子收咯

630 When the dessert has been eaten, take away the plates.

把水果,乾果,端來

631 Bring the fruit and nuts.

水果 SHUI³ GO³, lit., 'water fruit', fruit; 乾果 GAN¹ GO³, nuts, lit., 'dry fruit'.

煞角,把東西一下收了

632 Finally you may take everything away.

煞角 SHA² GO², finally, finished; the characters can scarcely be explained, but it is a well-known phrase found in the big dictionaries, and is in common use in speech.

把臺帕摺起、放在抽屜裏頭

633 Fold up the tablecloth and put it away in the drawer.

臺帕 TAI² PA⁴, tablecloth; 摺起 DJE² CHI³, to fold up; 抽屜 CHOU¹ TI², a drawer in table or any kind of furniture.

臺帕、要依倒原來的縐縐摺起

634 You must keep to the original crease in folding the tablecloth.

依倒 I¹ DAO³, according to; 縐縐 DZUNG⁴ DZUNG¹, crease, wrinkle; note change of tone in the second character of the duplication.

不可亂摺

635 You must not fold it regardless of the creases.

摺臺帕的時候、手要十分乾淨

636 When you fold the tablecloth, your hands must be perfectly clean.

十分 SHI² FEN¹, ten-tenths, *i.e.* perfect or perfectly.

王長興、這個話要緊

637 Wang Chang Hsin, this is a very important rule:

話 HWA⁴, word, words; here translated 'rule'.

弄飯的人,手要常常洗得乾乾淨淨的

638 The person who prepares food must have his hands always washed very very clean.

弄飯 LUNG[1] FAN[4], to prepare food, a very general expression; common.
Lit., "hands must always (be in the condition of) washed very clean".

LESSON 22. 第二十二課

弄 蛋

Cooking Eggs

弄 蛋

639 Cooking eggs.

弄 LUNG¹, to cook, to prepare, to repair; 蛋 DAN⁴, eggs. It is not necessary to say 鷄 蛋 GI¹ DAN⁴, hen's eggs, every time.

我們用的,盡都是雞蛋

640 We always use hen's eggs.

Lit., The we-use (eggs) entirely all are hen eggs. The whole phrase 我們用的 NGO³ MEN² YUNG⁴ DY², modifies the word, 蛋 DAN⁴ understood after 的 DY². 盡 DZIN⁴, entirely, wholly; 雞 GI¹, hen.

鴨蛋、鵝蛋、不買

641 You need not buy duck eggs or goose eggs.

鴨 蛋 YA² DAN⁴, duck eggs; 鵝蛋 WO² DAN⁴, goose eggs; 不 買 BU² MAI³, not buy, *i.e.* do not buy.

二則、陳蛋用不得

642 Furthermore, we cannot use stale eggs.

COOKING EGGS

二則 ER¹ DZE², in the second place, furthermore; 陳 CHEN², stale; 用不得 YUNG⁴ BU² DE², use not can, *i.e.* cannot be used.

要回回留心買新鮮的

643 You must pay close attention every time to the buying of fresh ones.

留心 LIU² SIN¹, pay attention; 新鮮 SIN¹ SIEN¹, fresh. as eggs or any other article of food. The character 鮮 SIEN¹ is also read SÜEN³, and in this sound and tone means few, rare, seldom.

早飯吃的蛋,輪流弄

644 Our breakfast eggs you are to prepare in various ways in turn.

Lit., Breakfast-eaten eggs in turn prepare. 輪流 LEN² LIU², in turn, by turns.

譬如,今天煮蛋

645 For instance, to-day you may boil the eggs.

譬如 PEI⁴ RU², for instance, for example; 煮 DJU³, to boil.

明天煎蛋

646 To-morrow you may fry the eggs.

煎 DZIEN¹, to fry.

後天炒蛋

647 Day after to-morrow, you may scramble the eggs.

炒 CHAO³, to scramble; this character really is another word meaning 'to fry' or 'to roast'; but since the food to be fried is usually well stirred in the process, this word comes about as near as any we can find to an equivalent of our 'scramble'.

萬後天煮開水蛋

648 The day after the day after to-morrow, you may poach the eggs.

萬後天 WAN⁴ HOU⁴ TIEN¹, the day after the day after to-morrow, a very convenient term in constant use; 煮 DJU³, to boil; 開水蛋 KAI¹ SHUI³ DAN⁴ hot water eggs, *i.e.* 'boil hot water eggs', poached eggs. This is a device to distinguish from the ordinary 煮蛋 DJU³ DAN⁴, to boil eggs in their shells. 煮開水蛋 DJU³ KAI¹ SHUI³ DAN⁴ is a foreign-made expression, but 煮荷包蛋 DJU³ HO² BAO¹ DAN⁴ is entirely Chinese colloquial, and may be preferred. Because the Chinese method of poaching eggs varies in different ways, the former expression has been introduced.

煮蛋就是煮渾的

649 (In order to) boil eggs, that is to boil them in the shell,

煮渾的 DJU³ KWEN² DY¹, boil whole, *i.e.* in the shell. The character 渾 here pronounced KWEN², is more often read HWEN¹, turbid, or HWEN² confused, chaotic. It is also used in speech in these senses and pronunciations. 649-652 make one long sentence.

先把水煮開

650 (you should) first bring the water to the boil,

煮開 DJU³ KAI¹, to boil open, to boil boiling, *i.e.* to bring to the boil.

COOKING EGGS

纔把蛋放下去

651 and then put the eggs in;

放下去 FANG⁴ HSIA⁴ CHÜ¹, to place go down go, *i.e.* 'to place down in the water'.

看倒鐘、煮三分半、就舀出來

652 watch the clock, boil them three minutes and a half, and then ladle them out.

看倒鐘 KAN⁴ DAO³ DJUNG¹, look at the clock; this sounds like an unnecessary injunction, but not for Chinese servants who are not used to doing things accurately, and who do not realize the value of half minutes. 三分半 SAN¹ FEN¹ BAN⁴, three minutes half; 舀 YAO³, to ladle.

蛋回回都要煑得嫩

653 Eggs should always be boiled soft.

嫩 LEN⁴, soft, tender. This word is applied to any kind of food, and to uncooked meat, for instance; also to live produce. *E.g.*, Buy a tender chicken, 買個嫩雞 MAI³ GO⁴ LEN⁴ GI¹.

煎蛋、先把平鍋坐熱

654 In frying eggs, you must first set the frying-pan (on the stove) till it is hot.

平鍋 PIN² GO¹, level fry-pan, *i.e.* the frying-pan, which has a flat level bottom instead of a deeply concave one like the Chinese 鍋 GO¹, fry-pan. 坐熱 DZO⁴ RE², to set hot, *i.e.* to set on the fire till it is hot.

放一點猪油,或奶油

655 Put in a little lard or butter.

猪油 DJU[1] YIU[2], pig oil, lard; 奶油 LAI[3] YIU[2], milk oil, butter.

把蛋,一個一個的打在茶船子頭

656 Break the eggs one by one into a saucer.

打 DA[3], to strike, to break open; 茶船子 CHA[2] CHWAN[2] DZ[3], saucer; 在......頭 DZAI[4]......TOU[2]: with 裏 LI[3] understood between, = inside.

不十分新鮮,就不要

657 Unless (they are) perfectly fresh, you must not use them.

不十分 BU[2] SHI[2] FEN[1], not ten-tenths, = not perfectly; 不要 BU[2] YAO[4], not want, the eggs are not wanted.

好的,就倒在平鍋裏頭

658 Empty the good ones into the frying-pan.

好的 HAO[3] DY[1], the good ones. 倒 DAO[4], to empty.

要不要的,鏟點油在蛋面上

659 Every now and again scoop a little of the grease on top of the eggs.

COOKING EGGS

鏟 CHWAN³, to shovel, because the Chinese cook uses a diminutive iron shovel for all such purposes, instead of a spoon; 點 DIEN³, a little; 油 YIU², oil, grease.

不要煎老咯

660 Do not fry them hard.

老 LAO³, hard, the opposite of 嫩 LEN⁴, tender, soft.

鏟在盤子上,端給人家

661 Lift them out on a plate and carry them to people.

鏟 CHWAN³, to shovel; we really should say 'shovel them out', because this is what the Chinese cook does; 端給人家 DWAN¹ GE¹ REN² GIA¹, carry to people.

炒蛋,先問共要幾個

662 (When you) scramble eggs, first ask how many are wanted altogether.

共 GUNG⁴, altogether.

譬如,要弄五個蛋

663 For instance if you wish to prepare five eggs,

把五個蛋,一個一個的打在茶船子頭

664 Take five eggs and break them one at a time into a saucer.

跟倒倒在大碗裏頭

665 Then empty them into a large bowl.

跟倒 GEN¹ DAO³, immediately, which is expressed with sufficient emphasis here by 'then'; 大碗 DA⁴ WAN³, a large bowl, such as is ordinarily used, by the Chinese as a vegetable bowl. The second 倒 is in the fourth tone, and means "to empty".

用乂子把蛋攪爛和勻淨

666 With a fork stir until they are broken and thoroughly mixed.

用乂子 YUNG⁴ CHA¹ DZ³, use fork, *i.e.* 'with a fork'; 攪 GIAO³, to stir; 爛 LAN⁴, broken; 和 HO⁴, to mix; 勻淨 YUIN² DZIN⁴, evenly, uniformly.

放一點鹽

667 Put in a little salt.

鹽 YEN², salt.

把平鍋熱起, 放油

668 Heat up the spider, and put in a little lard.

熱起 RE² CHI³, to warm up, to heat up; note the use of the adjective 熱 RE², warm, as a verb.

把一碗蛋倒在裏頭

669 Empty the bowl of eggs into it.

碗 WAN³, bowl, in this case becomes the classifier for 蛋 DAN⁴, eggs.

COOKING EGGS

趕緊攪

670 Quickly stir (them).

趕緊 GAN³ GIN³, quickly, hurry.

不歇氣的攪

671 Stir without cessation.

不歇氣的 BU² HSIE² CHI⁴ DY², lit:—'not rest breath', without stopping.

還不得老,就鏟出來,端給人家

672 Before they have become hard, ladle out and carry them to people (*i.e.* to those who are waiting at the table).

煮開水蛋

673 (To) poach eggs:

拿平鍋,倒一點水,煮開

674 Boil a little water in the frying-pan.

拿平鍋 LA² PIN² GO¹, get the frying-pan. This refers to a definite act, and differs markedly from the phrase 把平鍋 BA³ PIN² GO¹, which may ordinarily be translated 'take the frying-pan'. But this 'take the frying-pan' does not mean 'grasp the frying-pan', or 'take the frying-pan in one's hands'; it is rather merely an introduction to the remark following, as to what is to be done with the frying-pan. Try not to confuse these two classes of phrases.

把蛋、一個一個的打在茶船子頭

675 Break the eggs one at a time in a saucer. See 656 and 664.

好的、纔要

676 The good ones only are to be used.

陳的、不要

677 Stale ones are not to be used.

把蛋倒在開水裏頭

678 Empty the eggs into the boiling water.

把細、蛋黃不打爛

679 Be careful not to break the yolks.

蛋黃 DAN[4] HWANG[2], egg yellow, the yolk.

蛋煮合式的時候

680 When the eggs have been boiled as desired,

合式 HO[2] SHÏ[4], satisfactory, agreeable, suitable.

就舀出來

681 ladle them out.

COOKING EGGS

把水逼乾

682 Drain the water off (till they are) dry.

逼 BI², to drain off, as water from poached eggs, or from potatoes or other vegetables. 逼乾 BI² GAN¹, drain dry, a common phrase and useful in the kitchen. The character 逼 is borrowed for its sound and tone.

端來擺在棹子上

683 Carry them in and place on the table.

Why not use the one character 端 DWAN¹ here instead of 端來 DWAN¹ LAI²? We may say that the meaning is made more evident by the addition of the common word 來 LAI², come; but I believe that the main reason is after all the ever-present tendency to the dissyllabic word, as opposed to the monosyllabic. But here are action and reaction, for what is this tendency but the manifestation of the desire for perspicuity.

LESSON 23. 第二十三課

Cooking the Porridge

煮稀飯

煮稀飯

684 Cooking the porridge.

 煮 DJU³, to boil, to cook; 稀飯 HSI¹ FAN⁴, porridge; 'wet rice' originally, but applied by us to 'porridge'.

多一半用小麥熬稀飯

685 (We) mostly use wheat to prepare porridge.

 多一半 DO¹ I² BAN⁴, mostly, probably; 小麥 SIAO³ ME², wheat; 大麥 DA⁴ ME², barley; 玉麥 YÜ⁴ ME², corn.

用米或酒米,還是要得

686 Ordinary rice or glutinous rice also makes good porridge.

 米 MI³, ordinary rice, uncooked; 酒米 DZIU³ MI³, *lit.*, alcohol rice, commonly known as 'glutinous rice.' *Lit.*, 'Use ordinary rice or glutinous rice still is satisfactory.'

把小麥拿來淘乾淨

687 Bring the wheat and wash it clean.

COOKING THE PORRIDGE

淘 TAO[2], to scour or wash, as rice or wheat.

過後晒乾

688 Afterwards dry it in the sun.

Lit., Afterwards sun dry.

晒不得,就在爐子頭烤一下

689 In case you cannot sun it, then bake it in the oven for a little.

Lit., 'then in stove bake a little'. 烤爐 KAO[3] LU[2], bake stove, *i.e.* oven, not necessarily used here.

烤不倒好久一下

690 It must not be baked long,—just a few moments.

The addition of the 一下 I[2] HA[4], gives some indication that the time is to be very brief.

烤硬了,不好吃

691 If baked hard, it will not taste good.

硬 NGEN[4], hard. 不好吃 BU[3] HAO[3] CHĪ[2], not good eat, *i.e.* not tasty.

將將烤乾,就是了

692 Roast it until it is just dry, and that will be right.

將將 DZIANG[1] DZIANG[1], just exactly; 就是了 DZIU[4] SHĪ[4] LIAO[3], and that will be right or satisfactory.

用磨子推成粗麵

693   Grind it into coarse meal in the mill.
      Lit., With mill push become coarse flour.
      磨子 MO⁴ DZ³, mill; 推 TUI¹, to push, to turn a mill, etc. 粗 TSU¹, coarse; 麵 MIEN⁴, flour.

用罐子把水熬開

694   Bring water to a boil in a saucepan.
      罐子 GWAN⁴ DZ³, saucepan, jug, pitcher.

放一點鹽攪化

695   Put in a little salt and stir till dissolved.
      攪 GIAO³, to stir; 化 HWA⁴ to dissolve.

把麥麵抓一把來

696   Take up a handful of wheat meal.
      麥麵 ME² MIEN⁴, wheat meal, wheat flour; 抓 DJWA¹, to grasp in the hand; 一把 I² BA³, a handful.

慢慢的撽在開水裏頭

697   Let it run slowly through your fingers into the boiling water.
      慢慢的 MAN⁴ MAN⁴ DY¹, slowly, gradually; 撽 YEN⁴, to scatter a powder upon or into something, by allowing to fall from the fingers, as in this case, or as in salting food.

COOKING THE PORRIDGE

快很了，怕成籔籔

698 If you drop it too rapidly, I fear it will become lumpy.

籔籔 TO² TO¹, lumps. The second character rises into the first tone for euphony's sake.

籔籔不好吃

699 Lumps don't taste good.
See 691.

用大調羹攪勻淨

700 With a large spoon stir it till thoroughly mixed.
See 666.

現撒現攪

701 Keep stirring as you drop the meal in.

現……現 as……so; very common. Also 連路 lien lu……連路 lien lu; 里路 li lu……里路 li lu; 隨 sui……隨 sui; four methods of saying the same thing, but the first is most used.

麥麪不要撒多了

702 Do not drop too much meal in.

The sentence begins with 'wheat meal', the most important word in it.

稀飯釅了不對

703 Porridge that is too thick is not right.

釅了 NIEN³ LIAO³, too thick; also 'too strong' as tea.

稀了也不對

704　Neither is it right if too thin.

攪慣了，就弄得合式

705　When you have grown used to cooking it, you can make it satisfactory.

慣了 GWAN⁴ LIAO³, accustomed to; 攪慣了 GIAO³ GWAN⁴ LIAO³, 'accustomed to stirring', in which phrase the word 'stirring' is used for the whole process of cooking the porridge. 合式 HO² SHĬ⁴, satisfactory.

要長行攪，纔不得燒煳

706　You must stir constantly in order to avoid burning it.

燒煳 SHAO¹ FU², to 'heat to burning', *i.e.* to burn, as porridge, or any other kind of food.

煮一下，就趲到爐子後頭邊

707　Boil it for a little, and then move it to the back part of the stove.

趲 DZAN³, to move; 爐子 LU² DZ³, stove, here used for cook stove; 後頭邊 HOU⁴ TOU² BIEN¹, behind side, the back part.

儘他在那裡，慢慢煮

708　Let it stay there, and boil slowly.

儘他 DZIN³ TA¹, let it be, let it alone, a common phrase; this illustrates the rare instances in which 他 TA¹, is used in reference to a thing instead of a person.

COOKING THE PORRIDGE

天天下午,要照這個樣子

709 You are to do like this every afternoon:

下午 HSIA⁴ WU³, afternoon; 照 DJAO⁴, according to; 這個樣子 DJE⁴ GO⁴ YANG⁴ DZ⁴, this sort, this way.

把稀飯煮好

710 Boil the porridge until it is cooked.

拿蓋蓋阬嚴

711 Put the cover on tight.

蓋蓋 GAI⁴ GAI¹; 阬 KANG³, to cover up, as with a dish cover, this character is made by adding the mouth radical to the regular character 抗 KANG, and read in the third tone. That is to say, the *character* is made to fit the *word*. 嚴 NIEN², tight, close.

第二天清早,坐開

712 Next morning early, put it on the stove till it boils.

坐 DZO⁴, to set (as well as 'to sit'); 開 KAI¹, to boil, to come to the boiling point.

吃早飯的時候,就舀來擺起

713 At breakfast time ladle it out and place on the table.

LESSON 24. 第二十四課

送 信

Carrying a Letter.

送 信

714 Carrying a letter.

送 SUNG⁴, to carry, to send, to escort; 信 SIN⁴, a letter, a note.

趙興順，過來一下

715 Djao Hsin Shwen, come here a moment.

這裏有一封信

716 Here is a letter,

封 FUNG¹, classifier for letter,

要送到老關廟

717 (which) I want taken to Lao Gwan Miao,

交丁先生

718 and given to Mr. Din.

交 GIAO³, to deliver, to hand to.

CARRYING A LETTER

這個本本叫信本

719 This book is called a chit-book.

本本 BEN³ BEN³, book, usually used in reference to a note or pass book; 叫 GIAO⁴, called; 信本 SIN⁴ BEN³, letter book, chit book.

信夾在裏頭,看倒沒有

720 The letter is thrust in between the leaves of the book, do you see it?

夾 CHIA¹, to lay between two things, as a letter between leaves of a book. There is no character; this is borrowed to show meaning, and at the same time an approach to the sound.

把細,不要掉咯

721 Be careful not to lose it.

掉 DIAO⁴, to lose.

走攏的時候

722 When you arrive,

信本連信,交給看門的

723 give both letter and chit-book to the gateman.

連 LIEN², together with.

給他說是丁先生的信

724 Tell him that it is Mr. Din's letter.

先生，有沒得回信

725 Is there an answer?

  Asked by the coolie. 有沒得 YIU³ MU² DE², is there? 回信 HWEI² SIN⁴, return letter, answer.

那個話你不消問

726 You do not need to ask that;

  那個話 LA⁴ GO⁴ HWA⁴, that word, that matter; 消 SIAO¹, to need, to require.

把信本拿回來，就是了

727 just bring the chit-book home, and that will do.

有回信，他就夾在裏頭

728 (In case) there is an answer, he will lay it in the book.

  The 'in case' is understood. *Lit.,* 'he will lay it inside.'

請問先生，丁先生沒有在屋頭，怎麼樣

729 Will you please tell me what I should do in case Mr. Din is not at home?

  請問 TSIN³ WEN⁴, *lit.,* 'please ask,' a polite phrase to be used by any one when asking information; here used properly by the servant in speaking to his employer. 'In case' is understood, like 'if.' 怎麼樣 DZEN³ MO³ YANG⁴, what about

CARRYING A LETTER

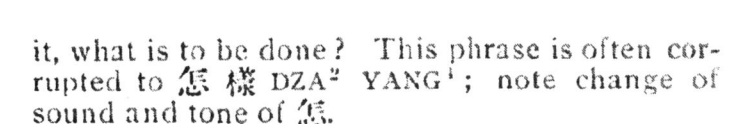

it, what is to be done? This phrase is often corrupted to 怎樣 DZA² YANG¹; note change of sound and tone of 怎.

丁先生沒有在屋頭

730 (If) Mr. Din is not at home,

在屋頭 DZAI⁴ WU² TOU¹, at home.

就可以把信拿出來

731 you may take the letter out,

交給看門的

732 and hand it to the gateman;

你把空信本拿回來，就算了

733 and you bring the empty chit-book home,—that's all.

空 KUNG¹, empty; 拿回來 LA² HWEI² LAI², to bring home; 算 SWAN⁴, to reckon, to calculate; 算了 SWAN¹ LIAO³, it is settled.

LESSON 25. 第二十五課

提燈籠送人
Carrying a Lantern for a Person

提燈籠送人
734 Carrying a lantern for a person.

提 TI², to carry, as one carries a lantern; 燈籠 DEN¹ LUNG⁰, a lantern; *lit.*, a lamp cage; 送 SUNG⁴, to attend, to accompany, to escort.

喊趙興順來
735 Call Djao Hsin Shwen to come.

趙興順，把燈籠點起
736 Djao Hsin Shwen, you may light the lantern.

點起 DIEN³ CHI³, to light, whether lamp, lantern, or the fire.

要同我一路到陝西街去
737 I want you to go with me to Shan Si Gai.

CARRYING A LANTERN FOR A PERSON

同我一路 TUNG² NGO³ I² LU⁴, with me; *lit.*, 'with me one road'; perhaps the very commonest form of expression with this meaning. 陝西街 SHAN³ SI¹ GAI¹, Shansi street.

走咯

738 Come on! or, We will start.
    See 316.

你在前頭打燈籠

739 You go in front with the lantern.

Lit., 'You in front strike lantern'; 打燈籠 DA³ DEN¹ LUNG², to carry the lantern.

慢點慢點,我掉了東西

740 Wait a minute, I have dropped something.

慢點 MAN⁴ DIEN³, *lit.*, 'a little slow', but its real meaning is 'a little more slowly', and in this sentence as translated, 'wait a minute', 'stop a minute'. 掉了 DIAO⁴ LIAO³, dropped, lost; DUNG¹ SI¹, things, something.

把燈籠提過來照一下

741 Bring the lantern over here and give me some light.

照 DJAO⁴, to light up, to illuminate.

找倒沒有

742 Have you found it?

找 DJAO³, to seek, to search, to find.

找倒咯

743 I have found it.

又走

744 We will go on again.

又走 YIU⁴ DZOU³, again go, again start.

趙興順、把細、不要撞倒人

745 Djao Hsin Shwen, be careful, don't bump into people.

撞 DJWANG⁴, to bump, to strike against.

些微離遠點子

746 (Carry the lantern) just a little farther away (from us),

些微 SI¹ WEI², a very little; this is the character 些 which forms the plural with 這 DJE⁴ and 那 LA⁴. In the sentence given here, it is pronounced in colloquial as SI¹, whereas when used to indicate the plural of pronouns, it is apt to get a HSIE¹ sound. In this sentence the 些 SI¹ is decidedly emphatic. 離 LI², to separate from, to be at a distance from; 遠 YUEN³, distant; 點子 DIEN³ DZ³, a little.

亮纔不熀眼睛

747 and then the light will not dazzle our eyes.

亮 LIANG⁴, a light; 熀 HWANG⁴, to dazzle; 眼睛 YEN³ DZIN¹, eyes.

CARRYING A LANTERN FOR A PERSON

攏了陝西街
748 We have arrived at Shan Si Gai.

可以把亮車小一點
749 You may turn the lantern down a little.

車 CHE¹, to turn; 小 SIAO³, small. In Chinese we do not turn the *lantern* down, but the *light*, which is quite logical.

不要吹熄
750 Do not blow it out.

吹 CHUI¹, to blow; the sound is perhaps nearer CHUE¹. 熄 SI², out, as a fire or flame.

等到我出來
751 Wait until I come out.

等 DEN³, to wait; 到 DAO⁴, to, till.

趙興順,走咯
752 Djao Hsin Shwen, we are going.

來了
753 I am coming.

This is shouted by the coolie in answer to the call in 752. Logically it is 'I have come', 'I have arrived'; but not so in actual use.

把亮車大一點
754 Turn the light up a little.

回去,不走來的那條路

755 In going home we shall not go the road we came.

回去 HWEI² CHÜ⁴, to go back, to go home; 來的那條路 LAI² DY² LA⁴ TIAO² LU⁴, lit., 'came that length road', i.e. 'the road we came'. 條 TIAO², length, the classifier for road, dog, street, etc.

我們耍走東大街,總府街,回去

756 We shall go home by the Great East Street and the Dzung Fu Street.

The whole verb is 走回去 DZOU³ HWEI² CHÜ⁴; it has been separated and the names of the two streets inserted between *dzou* and *hwei*.

倒拐嗎,端走

757 Do we turn (this) corner or go straight ahead?

倒拐 DAO³ GWAI³, to turn the corner; 端走 DWAN¹ DZOU³, straight go. i.e. go, straight on. The interrogative 嗎 MA¹ serves as usual as 'or'.

倒拐,倒拐

758 We turn here.
The repetition carries emphasis.

我怕把路走拐了

759 I am afraid we shall go the wrong road.

走拐了 DZOU³ GWAI³ LIAO³, to go wrong, as on a road.

CARRYING A LANTERN FOR A PERSON

不得錯、先生

760 There is no mistake.

Or this might be translated 'There can be no mistake'.

這個路有點轉、是不是

761 This road is a little roundabout, is it not?

轉 DJWAN⁴, to go round, to encircle; in the third tone, this character is constantly used in the sense of go or come back. 是不是 SHĬ⁴ BU² SHĬ⁴, is it not? Quite usable this way, but most often corrupted to SHĬ⁴ BU² SA².

只轉得倒半條街的樣子

762 It is longer by only about half a street.

只 GĬ³, only; 轉得倒 DJWAN⁴ DE² DAO³, to go around to the extent of; *i.e.* 'to be longer by'; 半 BAN⁴, half; 的樣子 DY² YANG⁴ DZ³, about. Compare 的光景 DY² GWANG¹ GIN³, same meaning, and placed at the end of sentence or clause, like this.

攏了屋頭了

763 We have arrived home.

The duplication of the 了 LIAO³, is part of the tendency seen so often, to make the meaning clear beyond a doubt, by some such means.

把燈籠提來交給我

764 Bring the lantern and give it to me.

我給你說一個法則

765　I want to tell you of a device;

　　　法則 FAH² DZE², device, method, plan.

燈籠火要車小

766　You must turn the lantern low;

　　　Lit:—'Lantern light turn small'.

車小的時候，他自己會熄

767　When you have turned it low, it will go out of itself.

　　　他 TA¹, it; very unusual to be applied to inanimate objects; 會 HWEI⁴, can, is able, is capable of; 熄 SI², to go out, going out.

不必吹熄

768　You do not need to blow it out.

　　　必 BI², necessary.

LESSON 26. 第二十六課

買 柴

Buying Firewood

買柴

769 Buying firewood.

王長興，今天可以出城買柴

770 Wang Chang Hsin, you are to go out of the city today to buy firewood.

出城 CHU² CHEN², to go out of the city. Note once more that the word expressing the time. 'today', is placed at the beginning of the sentence, except for the name of the servant called.

出東門外去講一下價

771 Go out to the East Gate suburb and talk prices for a little.

出東門 CHU² DUNG¹ MEN², to go out the east gate; the addition of the 外 WAI⁴, outside, indicates the place just outside, that is the suburb.

擔幾捆回來作樣子

772 Carry a few bundles back as samples.

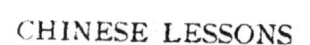

擔 DAN¹, to carry with shoulder-pole; 幾 GI³, several; 捆 KWEN³, a bundle, bundles; 作 DZO², to act as; 樣子 YANG⁴ DZ³, samples, patterns.

要松柴一捆青槓一捆

773　I want one bundle of pine, and one bundle of oak firewood.

松 SUNG¹, pine; 青槓 TSIN¹ GANG¹, oak.

松柴定要乾的一起

774　In the case of the pine firewood I must certainly have the dry sort.

定要 DIN⁴ YAO⁴, certainly must have, certainly want; 乾 GAN¹, dry, with 'firewood' understood after 的 DY². 一起 I² CHI³, one sort, one kind.

青槓乾嗎濕都不要緊

775　Whether the oak is dry or wet, is unimportant.

不要緊 BU² YAO⁴ GIN³, unimportant; 要緊 YAO⁴ GIN³, important.

樣子買回來了

776　The samples are bought and brought home.

這一起籤子多要七十八個錢一捆

777　For this kind with a large proportion of small stuff, they want seventy-eight cash a bundle.

BUYING FIREWOOD

The 'for' is understood. 籤子 TSIEN¹ DZ³, splinters, fine stuff, either split from large sticks, or the fine branches, brush, etc. 要 YAO⁴, i.e. 'they want', or 'there is wanted'.

這一起、盡是筒子、要一百一十個錢一捆

778 For this kind, which is all round stuff, they want one hundred and ten cash a bundle.

盡 DZIN⁴, all, entirely; 筒子 TUNG² DZ³, lit. tubes, round wood, unsplit, but much larger than the small twigs and brush included under 籤子 TSIEN¹ DZ³.

這青槓、盡是大塊子、要五個錢一斤

779 This oak is all in large sticks, and they want five cash a catty.

盡 DZIN⁴, all, entirely; 塊 KWAI³, a lump, a piece; this is the classifier for many words, as 一塊錢 I² KWAI³ TSIEN², one dollar.

柴價這麼高

780 Is the price of firewood so high?

柴價 CHAI² GIA⁴, firewood price; 這麼 DJE⁴ MO³, thus, so; 高 GAO¹, high. This sentence is, strictly speaking, exclamatory, not interrogative.

你走了幾處

781 To how many places did you go?

Li.t., 'You went how many places'?

我走咯四五個舖子，先生

782　I visited four or five shops.

　　Note that 咯 LO² and 了 LIAO³ seem to be interchanged indifferently.

很講了一陣價

783　I have argued prices for a good long time.

　　很 HEN³, very; 講了 GIANG³ LIAO³, argued, haggled; 一陣 I² DJEN⁴, a little while, a considerable time.

這一家纔合式一點

784　This was the only firm that was somewhat satisfactory.

　　After the preceding sentence, the words 這一家纔 DJE¹ I² GIA¹ TSAI², embody the idea that it was *only* this firm (*lit.*, 'family') that was 'a little' satisfactory. See 339.

那幾家貴得很

785　Those several firms were very dear.

　　很 HEN³, very, may precede, as in 783, or come at the end, as here.

這個柴就是相因的一起

786　This firewood is the very cheapest.

BUYING FIREWOOD

相因 SIANG¹ YIN¹, cheap; the commonest colloquial for this meaning. These charaters give sound and tone, but have no such meaning. After the verb 'to be', 是 SHĪ⁴, an adjective is almost always followed by the little particle 的 DY². 一起 I² CHI³, sort, one sort or kind.

明天又出城去
787 Tomorrow (you may) go out of the city again,

把幾挑柴買回來
788 to buy and bring home several loads of firewood.

買青槓,是不是包劃
789 In buying the oak, does (the price) include the splitting?

是不是 SHĪ⁴ BU² SHĪ⁴, is not is, does it or does it not; 包 BAO¹, to wrap up, to include; 劃 HWA¹, to split; this character is supposed to be in the second or fifth tone, but is always spoken in the first.

是包劃
790 It includes the splitting.

可以給他說
791 You may tell him.

要把柴劃細
792 (that I) want the firewood split fine,

纔好燒

793 so it will be convenient for burning.

燒 SHAO¹, to burn.

柴擔回來了

794 The firewood has been carried home.

王長興，把秤拿來

795 Wang Chang Hsin, bring the scales.

把青槓柴稱過

796 Weigh the oak firewood.

Lit., 'Take oak firewood and 'be after weighing it'.

把細稱，免得有錯

797 Be careful in weighing, lest you make a mistake.

免得 MIEN³ DE², lest; 有錯 YIU³ TSO⁴, there are mistakes.

王長興，把錢給咯算了

798 Wang Chang Hsin, pay the money and let us be done with it.

算了 SWAN⁴ LIAO³, it is reckoned, it is settled, let it go.

LESSON 27. 第二十七課

買 炭

Buying Coal.

買炭

799 Buying Coal.

    炭 TAN³, coal.

王長興,今天要買炭

800 Wang Chang Hsin, I want to buy coal today.

    It would be equally correct to translate this, 'I want you to buy coal today', or 'You are to buy coal today'.

可以買一挑回來作樣子

801 You may buy a load and bring it home as a sample.

    See 772.

價錢合式,石頭少

802 If the price is satisfactory, and not many stones in it,

    Lit., 'Price satisfactory, stones few', with 'if' understood.

我們給他多買一點

803 we will buy a considerable quantity from him.

給 GE[1], ordinarily 'to' or 'for', but here it is plainly 'from'. 多 DO[1], much, many. It is a curious idiom that makes this word, followed by 一點 I[2] DIEN[3] after the verb, mean 'more' instead of 'much'; that is to say 'we will buy more (than otherwise)'.

我們買煤炭,定要除皮

804 When we buy coal, we must certainly take out the weight of the container.

煤炭 MEI[2] TAN[4], the two-syllable word for coal, used always when there is need to distinguish from coke, charcoal, etc. 除皮 CHU[2] PI[2], take out or deduct container.

有一斤算一斤

805 A catty will reckon as a catty.

This is the most concise way of saying that we shall buy our coal by the catty, without any make-weight, such as baskets and ropes thrown in.

買炭回來了

806 The coal is bought and brought home.

把秤拿來

807 Bring the scales.

盡都要過吊

808 It must all be weighed.

BUYING COAL.

吊 DIAO⁴ to weigh, a colloquial word in rather more common use that 稱, CHEN¹ especially when the article to be weighed is large, bulky or heavy. 吊 DIAO⁴ also means 'to suspend'.

這一挑,重一百三十七斤

809 This load weighs one hundred and thirty seven catties.

Lit:— 'This load heavy 137 catties'.

不了,有一百四十幾

810 There are more than that; there are over one hundred and forty catties.

不了 BU² LIAO³, there is or there are more; it does not stop with that. A peculiar expression, but very convenient when one once becomes familiar with it.

我這個秤不得錯

811 These scales of mine are correct.

不得錯 BU² DE² TSO⁴, does not mean 'cannot be wrong', but simply 'are not wrong'.

是刀口天平秤

812 They are knife-edge standard scales.

刀口 DAO¹ KOU³, knife-mouth, *i.e.* knife-edge; 天平 TIEN¹ PIN², natural scales, *i.e.* standard scales, having exactly sixteen ounces to the catty, no more and no less.

又是較準了的

813　Furthermore they have been compared (with other scales) and accurately corrected.

又 YIU[4], also, furthermore; 較 GIAO[4], to compare, to try out, here read GAO[4]. 準 DJWEN[3], set, fixed, accurate. 'Scales' is understood after the 的 DY[2].

又稱一挑

814　Weigh another load.

你們兩個人的手拿開

815　You two men take your hands away.

Lit., 'You two men's hands take away'. 拿開 LA[2] KAI[1], take away, take out of the road.

身子離開点

816　Move your bodies away a little.

Lit., 'Bodies separate off a little'. 離開 LI[2] KAI[1], to leave, to separate.

這一挑只有一百三十五斤

817　This load is only one hundred and thirty five catties.

掌櫃你們這個炭不多好

818　Mr. Proprietor, this coal of yours is not very good.

BUYING COAL

掌櫃 DJANG³ GWEI⁴, proprietor, manager; 不多好 BU² DO¹ HAO³, 'not much good' i.e. 'not very good'. This may be varied to 不大好 BU² DA⁴ HAO³.

石頭太多了

819　There are too many stones.

多了 DO¹ LIAO³, too many; add the 太 TAI⁴, and the meaning is emphasized, 太多了 TAI⁴ DO¹ LIAO³, 'altogether too many'.

先生放心,有石頭包掉

820　Don't be disturbed, if there are stones I guarantee to exchange them (for good coal).

放心 FANG⁴ SIN¹, 'let your heart down' i.e. rest easy, be content; 'if' understood; 包 BAO¹, to guarantee, to take a contract for; 掉 TIAO⁴, to change, to exchange.

二回子有這麼多石頭,一概不收

821　Another time if there are so many stones, I shall decline to receive any of it.

二回子 ER⁴ HWEI² DZ³, a second time, another time; 這麼多 DJE⁴ MO³ DO¹, so many; 一概 I² KAI¹, the whole, all; 收 SHOU¹, to receive.

把炭擔進來倒

822　Carry the coal in and empty it.

把幾個筐筐重起過秤

823　Pile the several baskets together and weigh them.

　　筐 筐 KWANG¹ KWANG¹, baskets, a general term. 重 起 CHUNG² CHI³, to pile on top of; 過 秤 GO⁴ CHEN⁴, to pass over or through the scales, *i.e.* weigh them.

除了皮淨炭只有九百八十二斤

824　After deducting the containers, there are only nine hundred and eighty two catties clear coal.

　　淨 炭 DZIN⁴ TAN⁴, clean coal, *i.e.* coal without any make-weights.

王長興，你好生看倒他們抬炭的走

825　Wang Chang Hsin, you watch these coal-carriers carefully as they go out,

　　好 生 HAO³ SEN¹, careful, carefully; 他 們 抬 炭 的 TA¹ MEN² TAI² TAN⁴ DY¹, *lit.*, 'them the carry coal men' with 人 REN², understood after 的 DY². See 371.

免得他們把炭搋起走了

826　lest they carry coal away on their persons.

　　搋 CHWAI¹, to carry in the pocket or anywhere on the person.

BUYING COAL

掌櫃請在客廳頭坐一下

827 Mr. Proprietor, will you please sit down in the guest room for a moment,
   客廳 KE² TIN¹, guest room.

就把錢數給你

828 and I will count out the money for you.

LESSON 28. 第二十八課

洗 衣 裳

Washing Clothes

洗衣裳
829 Washing Clothes.

趙興順,今天要洗衣裳
830 Djao Hsin Shwen, you are to wash the clothes today.

每逢星期一就洗
831 You are to wash every Monday.
　　Lit., 'Every meet with Monday then wash'. 每 MEI[3], each; 逢 FUNG[2], to meet with, to occur.

把衣服端下樓
832 Carry the clothes down stairs.
　　端 DWAN[1] to carry, as a basket without a handle; 下 HSIA[4], to go down; 樓 LOU[2], a loft, an upper story, a tower.

把大鍋摻滿水
833 Fill the big boiler full of water.

WASHING CLOTHES.

鍋 GO[1]. the deep iron pan uniformly used by the Chinese for boiling or frying; 摻 TSAN[1], to add, to fill; 滿 MAN[3], full.

底下燒火

834 Start a fire beneath.

底下 DI[3] HSIA[4], below, beneath; 燒 SHAO[1], to burn; 火 HO[3], fire.

把這一塊胰子，切成片片丟在裏頭

835 Cut this piece of soap into slices and throw it in.

胰子 I[2] DZ[3], soap; 切 TSIE[2], to slice, to cut into slices; 成 CHEN,[2] to become, into; 片片 PIEN[4] PIEN[1], slices; 丟 DIU[1], to throw, to throw away. Note the change to the first tone, of the second 片 PIEN[4], for euphony; it is properly in the fourth.

把這麼多鹼，倒在裏頭

836 Empty this much (washing) soda into (the boiler).

鹼 GIEN[3], soda, potash, lye. This is a convenient word for washing soda, which acts by virtue of its alkaline properties.

把白的，給有顏色的衣裳，分開

837 (Now) separate the white and colored clothes.

白的 BE[2] DY[1], white, 'clothes' understood; 有顏色的 YIU[3] YEN[2] SE[2] DY[1], colored; *lit.*, 'have colors'; 分開 FEN[1] KAI[1], to separate. Note the use of 給 GE[1], and.

把白衣裳丟在鍋裏頭煮

838 Put the white clothes into the boiler and boil them.

衣裳 I¹ SHANG² is often spoken I¹ SHANG¹.

煮十幾二十分鐘,就拿起來

839 Boil (them) for ten to twenty minutes and then take them out.

拿起來 LA² CHI³ LAI², take out; *lit.,* 'take up', which in this case means taking them up out of the boiler.

丟在脚盆頭

840 Throw them into the tub.

脚盆 GIO² PEN², tub, of any sort; *lit.,* 'foot basin',

脚盆先裝半盆冷水

841 The tub must first be filled half full of cold water.

裝 DJWANG¹, to fill; 半 BAN⁴, half; 盆 PEN², basin, tub.

把搓板拿來,放在脚盆裏頭

842 Bring the washboard and place it in the tub.

WASHING CLOTHES.

搓板 TSO¹ BAN³ *lit.*, 'rub board', washboard.
搓 TSO¹, to rub between the palms, rub with the palms.

用胰子,把衣服一件一件的洗出來

843 Using soap, wash the clothes out garment by garment.

一件一件的 I² GIEN⁴ I² GIEN⁴ DY², one garment at a time.

好生洗,不要搓爛了

844 Be careful how you wash; do not rub (the garments) into holes.

爛了 LAN⁴ LIAO³, torn, rotten.

快把二個脚盆裝半盆水

845 Quickly fill another tub half full of water.

快 KWAI⁴, quick, quickly; 二個 ER⁴ GO⁴ another.

衣裳,隨洗出來,隨丟在二個脚盆頭

846 As the clothes are washed out, throw them into the other tub.

隨 SUI²...隨 SUI², as......so. See 168 and 701.

衣裳一件一件的清出來

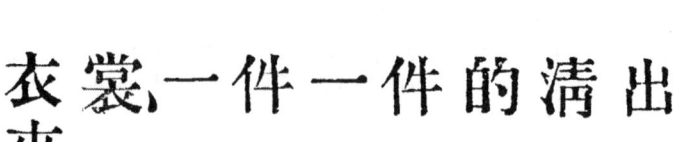

847 Rinse the clothes out, one garment at a time.
　　清 TSIN[1], to rinse.

又把第三個脚盆裝一點乾淨水

848 Again, take a third tub and put a little clean water into it.

下藍下去，使水有點藍色

849 Put in bluing until the water has a slight blue color.
　　下藍 HSIA[4] LAN[2], *lit.*, 'put the bluing down', *i.e.* put it down into the water. The two characters 下去 HSIA[4] CHÜ[4], are an example of the apparent redundancy of Chinese. It sounds very awkward, and probably about the best explanation is that "This is the way we speak" in China. The remainder of the sentence is literally "cause water have little blue color".

清出來的衣服要一件一件的透過藍水

850 You are to put the rinsed clothes through the blue water, one garment at a time. 透 TOU[4], to pass through.

WASHING CLOTHES

拿起來揪乾

851 Take them out and wring them dry.

See 159. This character 揪 is better for this purpose than 絞 given under 159; but even this has to have its tone changed from first to third.

搭在繩子上曬起

852 Hang them on the line to sun.

搭 DA², to place on or over an object, as a garment is hung over a line, or as a towel is hung on a towel-rack. 繩子 SHWEN² DZ³, rope, cord.

這下子,要洗有顏色的衣裳

853 Now then you are to wash the colored clothes.

趙興順,有個話要記穩當

854 Djao Hsin Shwen, here is something I want you to remember very carefully.

This is rather a free translation; 有一個話 YIU³ I² GO⁴ HWA⁴, lit., 'here is a word'; 穩當 WEN³ DANG⁴, firmly, solidly; 記 GI⁴, to remember.

顏色衣裳,萬煮不得

855 Colored clothes must not on any account be boiled.

萬 WAN⁴, ten thousand times; here an emphatic particle; 煮不得 DJU³ BU² DE², must not be boiled.

一煮就要脫色

856　On boiling they lose their color.

　　一煮 I² DJU³, lit., 'one boil', i.e. 'on boiling'; 脫 TO², to come off, to lose.

洗白衣裳的頭一盆水,不要倒

857　The first tub of water in which the white clothes were washed, is not to be thrown out.

　　頭一盆水 TOU² I² PEN² SHUI³, first one tub water. The first tub of water. The whole phrase 洗白衣裳的 SI³ BE² I¹ SHANG² DY², modifies the water 水 SHUI³, water, and the further phrase 頭一盆 TOU² I² PEN², comes in between, and also modifies the same word.

顏色衣裳放在這裏頭洗

858　Put the colored clothes into this to be washed.

還是用胰子搓

859　You are also to wash them with soap.

　　Lit., 'Still is use soap rub', *i.e.* wash with soap.

趲勁搓

860　Rub vigorously.

　　趲勁 DZAN³ GIN⁴, vigorously; *lit.*, 'urge strength'; a very common phrase and very useful.

WASHING CLOTHES

一件一件的洗乾淨
861 One by one wash (the clothes) clean.

跟倒清出來
862 Go right on with the rinsing,

  跟倒 GEN¹ DAO³, follow on, immediately.

像清白衣裳一樣
863 exactly as you rinsed the white clothes.

  像 CHIANG⁴, like, as; book pronunciation 'SIANG⁴', but constantly spoken CHIANG⁴. 一樣 I² YANG⁴, the same. 像 CHIANG⁴ and 一樣 I² YANG⁴ together give the meaning 'exactly' or 'exactly the same'.

不過藍水
864 They are not put through the bluing water.

拿起來揪乾
865 Take them out and wring dry.

拿去晾起,不晒
866 Hang them out to dry, but do not sun them.

晒咯怕變色
867 If they are put in the sun, one fears that they will change color, (*i.e.* fade).

  變 BIEN⁴, to change; 色 SE², color.

還有一個要緊的話

868 I have another important word (for you):

白的給顏色的,萬不可和倒洗

869 white and colored clothes must not under any circumstances be washed together.

和倒 HO⁴ DAO³, to mix together.

怕把白的染花了

870 One fears that the white clothes would become streaked with color.

染 RAN³, to dye; 花了 HWA¹ LIAO³, streaked; *lit.*, 'flowered'. See 169.

白衣裳,有人先洗後煑

871 Some people first wash their white clothes, and boil them after.

我們肯先煑後洗

872 We prefer to boil them first, washing after.

肯 KEN³, to be willing; here 'to prefer'.

那個法則慼脫,那個法則好

873 Whatever method is most convenient, that we shall use.

WASHING CLOTHES

Both characters 那 LA³ are in the third tone. 法則 FA² DZE², method; 憋脫 PIE² TO², convenient; a very much used colloquial word; the characters are adapted to this meaning. This sentence is literally:—'Whichever method convenient, whichever method then good', in which we see the superlative sense, given in the free translation as 'most convenient'.

總圖把衣裳洗得乾淨

874 The chief object is to secure the washing of the clothes clean.

總 DZUNG³, emphatic particle, 'certainly', 'in any case'; 圖 TU², to covet, to desire.

又不要扯爛

875 And we don't want them torn.

又 YIU⁴, also, here 'and'; 扯 CHE³, to pull; 爛 LAN⁴, torn; 扯爛 CHE³ LAN⁴, to tear.

LESSON 29. 第二十九課

熨衣裳
Ironing

熨衣裳
876 Ironing.

    熨 YUIN^1, to iron, a flat-iron.

硬領紿袖口,要用外國漿粉漿

877 For cuffs and stiff collars, you are to use foreign starch.

    硬 NGEN^4. stiff, hard; 領 LIN^3, collars; 袖口 SIU^4 KOU^3, cuffs; *lit.*, 'sleeve mouth'; 外國 WAI^4 GWE^2, foreign; *lit.*, 'outside country'; this term is entirely polite and respectful and may be used in reference to either persons or things; this can hardly be said of the term 洋 YANG^2, perhaps because a disrespectful meaning has been put into it during these first decades of intercourse with foreigners. 漿粉 DZIANG^4 FEN^3, starch powder; 漿 DZIANG^1, to starch. Note different tones for noun and verb.

除此以外,用米湯漿

878 Otherwise you may use rice water for starching.

    除 CHU^2, to take out; 此 TSI^3, this; same as 這個 DJE^4 GO^4, but more bookish. 以外 I^3

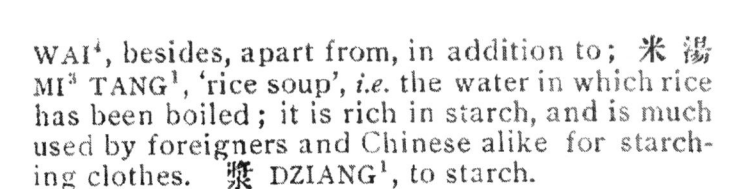

IRONING

WAI[4], besides, apart from, in addition to; 米湯 MI[3] TANG[1], 'rice soup', *i.e.* the water in which rice has been boiled; it is rich in starch, and is much used by foreigners and Chinese alike for starching clothes. 漿 DZIANG[1], to starch.

沒得米湯,就用荳粉,也使得

879 If there is no rice water, then you may use bean powder.

荳 DOU[4], beans; 粉 FEN[3], powder. The last three characters, 也使得 YE[3] SHI[3] DE[2], 'also will do' are not necessarily translated here.

漿好了,又要晒乾

880 When you have finished the starching, then sun them dry again.

晒乾了,要拿來灑水

881 When they are dry, then sprinkle water on them.

灑 SA[3], to sprinkle. *lit.*, 'Sun dried want bring sprinkle water'.

一件一件的打開,鋪在棹子上

882 Open them out garment by garment, and spread them on the table.

打開 DA[3] KAI[1], to open, the most common expression for this English verb. 鋪 PU[1], to spread out.

用手洒水,不要口噴

883 Use your hand to sprinkle water, do not spray with your mouth.

噴 FEN⁴, to spurt water or any other liquid from the mouth. The addition of 口 KOU³ to 噴 FEN⁴ makes the word into a dissyllable, and adds greatly to clearness.

決不可用口噴

884 You must not under any circumstances spurt water with your mouth.

決 DJUE², a particle expressing great emphasis.

洒水,要洒勻淨

885 In sprinkling water, you must sprinkle evenly.

勻淨 YUIN² DZIN⁴, evenly.

要不多不少的,合式就是咯

886 You must not (sprinkle) too much or too little, but just a sufficient amount.

lit., 'Want not much not less, suitable, and that's all'. The word 水 SHUI³, water, is understood after 的 DY². The two characters 不多 BU² DO² and 不少 BU² SHAO³, while literally meaning 'not much' and 'not less' have really the meaning of 'not too much' and 'not too little'.

IRONING

洒過後,就一件一件的裹起

887 After sprinkling, then roll them up garment by garment.

洒 SA³, to sprinkle; 過後 GO⁴ HOU⁴, afterwards; 裹 GO³, to roll up.

裹緊撿一下

888 Roll them tight, and put them away for a while.

緊 GIN³, tight, firm.

三把熨斗,擱在灶高上,燒熱

889 Put the three flat-irons on the stove and heat them hot.

熨斗 YUIN⁴ DOU³, flat-irons; 燒熱 SHAO¹ RE² to warm up, to heat up, to make hot.

不要燒熱很了

890 Do not make them too hot.

熱很了 RE² HEN³ LIAO³, too hot.

在紙上試一下,看燙得糊,燙不糊

891 Try them a little on paper, to see whether they will scorch or not.

紙 GI³, paper; 試 SHI⁴, to try, to examine, to make experiment; 燙 TANG⁴, to scorch, to scald, to burn; 煳 FU², to burn food in cooking, to burn brown or black, to scorch. 燙得煳 TANG⁴ DE² FU², it will burn brown; 燙不煳 TANG⁴ BU² FU², it will not burn (things).

燙不煳,纔要得

892 It should not burn (things) in order to be satisfactory.

這幾樣可以不洒水,乾熨

893 These several garments you must not sprinkle, but iron dry.

這幾樣 DJE⁴ GI³ YANG⁴, these several kinds, which may therefore include articles that are not garments. 乾熨 GAN¹ YUIN⁴, dry iron.

先熨這幾樣

894 You may iron these things first,

We are most apt to put the word 'first' at the end, as here, whereas in Chinese we put it at the beginning of the sentence.

熨完了,纔把潤的拿出來熨

895 When you have finished ironing these, then bring out the damp things and iron them.

潤 RWEN⁴, damp, dampness; 潤的 RWEN⁴ DY², the damp ones, or damp things or garments.

IRONING.

好生熨伸展

896 Be careful to iron things out smooth.

伸展 CHEN[1] DJAN[3], straight, smooth, without wrinkles.

不要起縐縐

897 Do not get them wrinkled.

起 CHI[3], to rise up, to cause to rise up; 縐縐 DZUNG[4] DZUNG[1], wrinkled; properly DZOU[4], but corrupted in West China to DZUNG[4]. Note change in second character to first tone, for euphony.

件件要熨乾

898 One by one iron them dry.

熨斗囬囬要擦得乾乾淨淨的

899 You must rub your irons perfectly clean every time.

擦 TSA[2], to rub one article with another, as opposed to 搓 TSO[1], to rub with the palms. Note the position of the 囬囬 HWEI[2] HWEI[2], adverb of time, at the beginning of the sentence, except for the noun,

免得把衣裳熨髒了

900 lest you dirty the clothes with them.

免得 MIEN[3] DE[2], lest; 熨髒了 YUIN[4] DZANG[1] LIAO[3], to iron them dirty, i.e. to dirty them with the irons.

熨斗溫熱的也不對

901 If your irons are only slightly warm, neither will they be satisfactory.

   溫熱 WEN[1] RE[2], lukewarm, especially as applied to water.

熨不伸, 熨不乾

902 (In that case) you cannot iron things either smooth or dry.

   lit., 'Iron not smooth, iron not dry'.

熨的時候, 要按得重, 纔要得

903 While ironing, you should press down heavily.

   按 NGAN[4], to press down; 重 DJUNG[4], heavily, heavy. The last three characters 纔要得 TSAI[2] YAO[4] DE[2], are not necessarily translated.

擱熨斗, 要擱穩當

904 When you put your iron down, you should place it firm.

趖下去, 怕欛子打斷

905 If it slides off to the floor, I fear the handle will be broken.

   趖 SO[1], to slide, to slip down or off; 欛子 BA[3] DZ[3], a handle; 斷 DWAN[4], to break in two; 打斷 DA[3] DWAN[4], to 'strike broken', *i.e.* to break in two.

LESSON 30. 第三十課

睡 房

The Bedroom

睡房

906 The Bedroom.

睡 SHUI⁴, to sleep; 房 FANG², room, house.

趙興順,可以上樓來,打整睡房

907 Djao Hsin Shwen, you may come upstairs and put the bedroom to rights.

上樓來 SHANG⁴ LOU² LAI², to come upstairs; 打整 DA³ DJEN³, to put to rights.

把燈端下樓去

908 Carry the lamp down stairs.

洗臉盆裏外擦乾淨

909 Wash the wash-basin clean, inside and out.

洗臉盆 SI³ LIEN³ PEN², wash-basin; *lit.,* 'wash face basin'. 裏外 LI³ WAI⁴, inside (and) outside; 擦 TSA², to rub, with a cloth for instance; freely translated as 'wash'.

胰子盒盒,洗乾淨

910 Wash the soap-dish clean.

盒盒 HO² HO¹, any little dish or box, whether round or square, with a cover that *lifts* off, as opposed to *sliding* off. Note change of tone in the second *ho*.

髒水桶,提下去倒

911 Carry the slop-pail down and empty it.

髒水桶 DZANG¹ SHUI³ TUNG³, slop-pail; *lit.*, 'dirty water pail'.

髒水桶洗乾淨,搣乾,提來還原

912 Wash the slop-pail clean, wipe it dry, and then put it back in its place.

搣乾 MA² GAN¹, to wipe dry; 提來 TI² LAI², to carry come, *i.e.* to bring; 還原 HWAN² YUEN², to put back.

這下子,可以理床鋪

913 Now you may make the bed.

理 LI³, to put in order; 床鋪 CHWANG² PU¹, a general term for bed and bedding.

枕頭,鋪盖,臥禪,一下拿開

914 Take the pillows, quilts, and sheets all off the bed.

THE BEDROOM

枕頭 DJEN³ TOU², pillows; 鋪盖 PU¹ GAI¹, quilts; 臥襌 WO⁴ DAN¹, sheets.

不要丢在地下,放在椅子上

915 Do not throw them on the floor; put them on the chairs.

墊的那一床臥襌,拿出去抖一下

916 Take the under sheet outside and shake it.

墊的那一床臥襌 DIEN⁴ DY¹ LA⁴ I² CHWANG² WO⁴ DAN¹, the under sheet; *lit.*, 'underneath, that one sheet.' 抖 TOU³, to shake.

墊的那床鋪盖,理伸

917 Smooth the under quilt out properly.

伸 CHEN¹, straight, smooth.

把綿臥襌,絨臥襌,鋪盖,面襌,挨一挨二的鋪起

918 Spread the cotton sheets, blankets, quilts and coverlet on the bed in their proper order.

綿臥襌 MIEN² WO⁴ DAN¹, cotton sheets; 絨臥襌 RUNG² WO⁴ DAN¹, woolen sheets, *i.e.* blankets; 面襌 MIEN⁴ DAN¹, coverlet; 挨一挨二的 NGAI¹ I² NGAI¹ ER⁴ DY², in regular order; 鋪 PU¹, to spread out or on.

墊的臥襌、四方的邊邊、要搌進去

919 The under sheet is to be tucked in on all four sides.

四方 SĪ⁴ FANG¹, four sides; 邊邊 BIEN¹ BIEN¹, edges; 搌 DJAN³, to tuck in; this *word* is familiar and very common, but this *character* is borrowed for its sound and tone, having no such meaning of itself.

蓋的幾床、要挨次序擺起

920 The several upper covers are to be put on in order.

This sentence is the same as 918, except that the different covers are not named. The purpose of inserting it is to get two or three slightly different terms. 挨次序 NGAI¹ TSĪ⁴ HSÜ⁴, is another way of saying 'in regular order', and is exactly, the same as 挨一挨二的 NGAI¹ I² NGAI¹ ER⁴ DY², 擺 BA⁴, and 鋪 PU¹, are very similar; 鋪 PU¹, lays a little more emphasis on the spreading out smooth; whereas 擺 BA⁴, emphasizes laying something down on something else, and making it firm or comfortable for sleeping.

不要攪亂了

921 Don't get them mixed.

攪 GAO³, to cause, to allow; this character is adapted to this word; it is in the right tone, but the sound has had to be changed from GIAO³ to GAO³. In this pronunciation the word is very common.

THE BEDROOM

一床一床的攞伸

922 One by one lay them on smooth.

不要縐起

923 Do not get them wrinkled.

面禪,底脚搌進去,兩邊吊起

924 Tuck in the coverlet at the foot, but allow the two sides to hang down.

底脚 DI³ GIO², 'below foot', *i.e.* the foot; 吊起 DIAO⁴ CHI³, to hang down.

枕頭,擱來嗙起

925 Place the pillows in a leaning position.

擱來 KO⁴ LAI², 'place come', *i.e.* to place; 嗙 PEN¹, to lean, to incline to one side or against something; this character gives the correct sound, but the tone has had to be changed to first, and the mouth radical is added to indicate that it is a borrowed character.

擱好了,把枕頭套子理伸

926 When you have placed the pillows properly, smooth out the pillow-slips.

枕頭套子 DJEN³ TOU² TAO⁴ DZ³, pillow-slips.

罩子,白天搭起來

927 The mosquito net is to be thrown up over the frame by day.

罩子 DJAO⁴ DZ³, the net; also 'lamp globe' or 'lamp shade'. 搭起來 DA² CHI³ LAI², to place on or over or on top of.

這一雙鞋子,拿去擦乾淨刷墨

928 Take this pair of boots away, brush them clean, and put on blacking.

鞋子 HAI² DZ³, boots, shoes; 擦 TSA², to rub, to brush; 刷 SHWA², to brush with a brush; 墨 ME². ink, blacking.

要刷亮,纔好看

929 Polish them and then they will look nice.

SHWA² LIANG⁴, to brush until they shine.

架子上的乾帕子,要理伸

930 Arrange the towels neatly on the towel-rack.

架子 GIA⁴ DZ³, a frame or rack; 乾帕子 GAN¹ PA⁴ DZ³, towels; *lit.*, 'dry cloths'; 理伸 LI³ CHEN¹, to arrange in order or 'unfolded'.

地下的氈子,要拿出去抖

931 The rugs on the floor are to be taken out and shaken.

THE BEDROOM

氈子 DJAN[1] DZ[3], mats, rugs; 抖 TOU[3], to shake.

不忙拿進來,放在外頭

932 Don't be in a hurry to bring them in; leave them outside.

不忙 BU[2] MANG[2], not hurry, don't hurry, no hurry; 放在外頭 FANG[4] DZAI[4] WAI[4] TOU[2], place them outside, but here translated more freely as 'leave them outside'. Notice the duplication of expression, on the same principle so often noted heretofore, of the duplication of words, in order to make absolutely sure of the meaning.

跟倒掃地

933 Then sweep the floor.

跟倒 GEN[1] DAO[3], at once, immediately after.

等到灰定了纔㨉灰

934 Wait until the dust has settled before dusting.

灰 HWEI[1], dust; 定了 DIN[4] LIAO[3], fixed, settled.

把大鏡子㨉乾淨

935 Wipe the big mirror clean.

鏡子 GIN[4] DZ[3], mirror.

把梳子,筐子,衣服刷子,擺歸一

936 Place the comb, hair-brush and clothes-brush in order.

梳子 SU¹ DZ³, comb, a coarse comb; 筅子 MIN³ DZ³, hair-brush; 衣服刷子 I¹ FU² SHWA² DZ³, clothes-brush; 擺 BAI³, to spread out; 歸一 GWEI¹ I², neatly, in order,

把梳粧臺洗臉櫃上的各樣東西,理歸一

937 Put all the articles on the dresser and washstand in order.

梳粧臺 SU¹ DJWANG¹ TAI², dresser; 洗臉櫃 SI³ LIEN³ GWEI⁴, washstand; *lit.*, 'wash-face-cupboard'.

煞角洗地,就歸一了

938 Finally wash the floor and all will be finished.

煞角 SHA² GO², finally, finished.

LESSON 31. 第三十一課

洗澡房
The Bathroom

洗澡房

939 The Bathroom.

澡 DZAO³, to bathe, to bathe the body. Therefore 洗澡 SI³ DZAO³ is a duplication of words having the same or very similar meanings.

趙興順,過來一下

940 Djao Hsin Shwen, come here a moment.

我給你說這個小脚盆,長行要洗乾淨,嗙起

941 Listen to me: this small tub is to be always kept washed clean, and leaning (up against the wall).

我給你說 NGO³ GE¹ NI³ SHO², I to you say, *i.e.* 'I tell you'; here translated more freely as 'Listen to me'. 脚盆 GIO² PEN², a tub; 嗙 PEN¹, to lean against, to incline against. See 925.

洗澡盆,要天天早上把髒水舀去倒

942 Every morning you are to ladle the dirty water

out of the bath tub, and take it away and empty it.

洗澡盆 SI³ DZAO³ PEN², bath tub; 髒水 DZANG¹ SHUI³, dirty water; 舀 YAO³, to ladle out; 去 CHÜ⁴, go; here it answers for the longer phrase 'take it away'.

跟倒把盆子洗乾淨

943 Then immediately wash the bath tub clean.

提兩桶乾淨水,倒在裏頭

944 Bring two pails of clean water and empty them into it;

我好天天早上洗冷水澡

945 so that I may conveniently take a cold bath each morning.

好 HAO³, conveniently; 洗冷水澡 SI³ LEN³ SHUI³ DZAO³, to take a cold bath.

每逢禮拜日的清早,要燒一桶滾水

946 I want you to heat a pail of water very hot every Sunday morning.

禮拜日 LI³ BAI⁴ RÏ², Sunday; one of the best terms for Sunday; also may be called 主日 DJU³ RÏ², and 星期日 SIN¹ CHI¹ RÏ², or simply 星期 SIN¹ CHI¹. 清早 TSIN¹ DZAO³, very early, 燒 SHAO¹, to burn, to heat; 滾 GWEN³, very hot; not necessarily boiling.

THE BATH-ROOM

燒開,更好

947 If you heat it to boiling, so much the better.

燒開 SHAO¹ KAI¹, 'burn open', i.e. 'heat to boiling'; 更好 GEN⁴ HAO³, lit., 'more good' i.e. better.

提上來擱倒,喊我一聲

948 Carry it upstairs, put it down, and give me a call;

喊我一聲 HAN³ NGO³ I² SHEN¹, lit., 'call me one voice'.

我好起來洗熱水澡

949 so that I may get up and take a hot bath.

好 HAO³, conveniently; here sufficiently translated in the phrase 'so that I may'. 洗熱水澡 SI³ RE² SHUI³ DZAO³, lit., 'wash hot water bath'.

這個小爐子,長行耍架起柴

950 I want you to always have firewood laid in this small stove.

架 GIA⁴, to lay, as firewood for a fire. This character as a noun means 'frame' or 'rack'; see 930. 柴 CHAI², firewood.

你看倒火燃過的時候

951 When you see that there has been a fire,

Lit., 'You see fire burned when', the relative adverb 'when' at the end of the phrase as usual.
燃 RAN², to blaze; 燃過 RAN² GO⁴, burned, burned out.

就把爐子打整乾淨，又架起柴

952　then clean the stove and again lay firewood.

　　打整 DA³ DJEN³, to put to rights, to set in order; 打整乾淨 DA³ DJEN³ GAN¹ DZIN⁴, to make thoroughly clean.

洗澡房的地陣，天天要洗

953　You are to wash the floor of the bathroom every day.

乾帕架子要搣灰

954　Dust the towel-rack.

　　乾帕 GAN¹ PA⁴, towels; 架子 GIA⁴ DZ³, rack.

洗澡房的零碎東西，理歸一

955　Arrange neatly all the miscellaneous articles of the bathroom.

　　零碎 LIN² SUI⁴, odds and ends, miscellaneous.

LESSON 32. 第三十二課

喂 牛
Keeping a Cow

喂 牛

956 Keeping a cow.

喂 WEI⁴, to feed; 牛 NIU², a cow; 喂牛 WEI⁴ NIU², *lit.*, 'to feed a cow', *i.e.* to keep a cow.

趙興順,我們要買一根牛,擠奶子

957 Djao Hsin Shwen, we want to buy a cow to milk.

根 GEN¹, the most usual classifier for 'cow'; 擠 DZI³, to squeeze; 擠奶子 DZI³ LAI³ DZ³, to 'squeeze milk', *i.e.* 'to milk'.

你認得來牛嗎

958 Do you know a good cow?

Lit., 'Do you know cows?' 認得 REN⁴ DE², to know, to recognize. 認得來 REN⁴ DE² LAI², to have the ability to recognize.

認得來

959 Yes, I can distinguish a good cow.

好，你可以下鄉去找

960 Good; you may go into the country to look for one.

下鄉 HSIA⁴ SIANG¹, to go into the country; *lit.*, 'to go down into the country'; the verb is not really complete without the 去 CHÜ⁴ which immediately follows the 鄉 SIANG¹, although the phrase 下鄉 HSIA⁴ SIANG¹, is constantly spoken by itself. 找 DJAO³, to search.

要纔下過兒子的牛，纔好

961 I want a cow that has recently borne a calf.

纔 TSAI², just, recently; 下 HSIA⁴, to give birth to; to lay, as eggs, as 下蛋 HSIA⁴ DAN⁴; 過 GO⁴, expresses past tense, or completed action; 兒子 ER² DZ³, 'son' ordinarily, but here 'the young' of an animal. The particular animal is clearly expressed by the occurrence of the 牛 NIU² in the sentence.

牛兒子有一兩個月就合式

962 If the calf is one or two months old, that will be satisfactory.

Lit., "Calf has one or two months, then satisfactory".

第一要緊要看牛的奶包大

963 It is of first importance to see that the cow's udder is large.

KEEPING A COW

第一 DI⁴ I², first; 要緊 YAO⁴ GIN³, important; 奶包 LAI³ BAO¹, udder.

奶頭、又耍長大

964 Her teats also should be long and large.

奶頭 LAI³ TOU², teats, nipples.

牛架子大、肥一點、不瘦

965 The cow should be large in body, and rather fat, not lean.

架子 GIA⁴ DZ³, frame or framework; 肥 FEI², fat; used of lower animals, never of persons; 瘦 SOU⁴, lean, thin.

牛耍嫩點、不過幾歲、纔好

966 The cow should be rather young, certainly not over ten years of age.

嫩 LEN¹, tender, young; 點 DIEN³, a little, rather; 不過 BU² GO⁴, only, not more than; 幾歲 GI³ SUI⁴, several years of age, *i.e.* under ten.

像這宗牛、奶子該多

967 A cow like this should have plenty of milk.

lit., 'Like this sort cow, milk ought much'. 像 CHIANG⁴, like, similar to; usually READ SIANG⁴ but SPOKEN CHIANG⁴. 該 GAI¹, ought; constantly so used, meaning 'ought to be', 'should be'. It is also much used in another familiar sense meaning 'belonging to', as 該不該他 GAI¹ BU² GAI¹ TA¹, does it belong to him?

找倒這樣的牛,可以把價講定

968 When you find this kind of a cow, you may argue the price and fix it.

'When' is understood. 價 GIA⁴, price; 講 GIANG³, to argue, as a price. This is also the common character meaning 'to preach'; 定 DIN⁴, fixed, determined; 講定 GIANG³ DIN⁴, to argue prices and come to an agreement.

限三十塊錢,有少嗎,更好

969 I shall limit you to thirty dollars; if you can get the cow for less, so much the better.

限 HSIEN⁴, to limit, a limit.

講成了,可以交一元定錢

970 When you have come to an agreement, you may pay one dollar as earnest money.

講成 GIANG³ CHEN², to argue until the bargain is completed; very similar to 講定 GIANG³ DIN⁴. 定 DIN⁴ is 'fixed' whereas 成 CHEN² is 'completed'. 交 GIAO¹, to hand over, to pay over, to deliver to; 一元 I² YUEN², one dollar; 定錢 DIN⁴ TSIEN², earnest money.

要把牛牽回來,喂幾天

971 I want you to lead the cow home, where we shall keep her for a few days.

KEEPING A COW

牽 TSIEN[1], to lead, as a cow or a dog; 喂 WEI[4], to feed, used in the sense of 'keep' here.

賣牛的,來一個人經佑牛還是使得

972 If the seller of the cow will send a man along to look after her, that will be all right.

賣牛的 MAI[4] NIU[2] DY[1], the seller of the cow; 來一個人 LAI[2] I[2] GO[4] REN[2], 'come one man', 'a man may come' *i.e.* from the family of the seller. 經佑 GIN[1] YIU[1], to look after, to care for,

牛兒子小了,走不得,可以背

973 If the calf is small and unable to walk, you may carry it on your back.

小了 SIAO[3] LIAO[3], too small; 走不得 DZOU[3] BU[2] DE[2], cannot walk; 背 BEI[1], to carry on the back; this character read in the fourth tone is the noun, 'back'.

拿這塊錢去,作定錢

974 Take this dollar for use as earnest money.

作 DZO[2], 'to act as', 'for use as'.

拿兩吊錢作盤川

975 Take two thousand cash as travelling expenses.

盤川 PAN[2] CHAN[1], travelling expenses. The character 川 here pronounced CHAN[1] is borrowed for this use. It is of course properly CHWAN[4] and means 'streams'; 四川 SZECHWAN, the 'Four Streams' province; but it gives the correct *tone*, though not the correct *sound* for this word. Similarly the character 纏 CHAN² which is used in some books for this word, gives the correct sound but is incorrect for tone. Therefore you may please yourself which one of these two characters you make use of. Get the *spoken word* right, whatever you do about the character!

牛給牛兒子,牽回來了

976 Cow and calf have been led home.

大牛,拴在牛圈頭

977 Tie the cow in the cowstable.

大牛 DA⁴ NIU², the cow,—when wishing to distinguish from the calf. 拴 SHWAN¹, to tie; 圈 GÜEN⁴, a pen for animals; 牛圈 NIU² GÜEN⁴, cowstable.

牛兒子,放兩天,僅他吃奶子

978 Set the calf free for a couple of days, and let it have the milk.

放 FANG⁴, to set free; 僅 GIN³, to let, to allow; 吃奶子 CHĪ² LAI³ DZ³, to 'eat milk', exactly as we say 吃茶 CHĪ² CHA², 'to eat tea' when we mean 'to drink tea'.

大牛,每天要喂幾十斤草

979 The cow is to be fed several tens of catties of grass daily.

Note the idiom; first the article or thing talked about,—the cow; then the *time*; and finally the remark that is made about this subject.

KEEPING A COW

又要喂兩升麩子

980 She is also to be fed two shen of bran.

升 SHEN¹, a tenth of the 斗 DOU³ or bushel; 麩子 FU¹ DZ³, bran.

這下子,兩天過了,可以把牛兒牽開

981 Now the two days have gone by, and you may tie the calf away from its mother.

拴開 SHWAN¹ KAI¹, 'tie separate' *i.e.* tie away from the cow.

趙興順,你來看倒我擠奶子

982 Djao Hsin Shwen, come and watch me milk.

看過幾回,看你學得會嗎

983 After you have watched me a few times, we shall see whether you can learn how.

lit., "Seen several times, (we shall) see you learn can able?" 幾回 GI³ HWEI², several times, a few times; 學得會 HSIO² DE² HWEI⁴, can you learn how? Similarly 學不會 HSIO² BU² HWEI⁴, I cannot learn how.

可以端一盆乾淨溫熱水出來

984 You may bring out a basin of clean warm water.

温熱 WEN¹ RE², warm, lukewarm.

又要乾淨帕子

985 You must also have a clean cloth.

可以把奶包、奶頭、洗得乾乾淨淨的

986 You are to wash the udder and teats very, very clean.

怕他踢人，不敢去洗

987 I fear she will kick; I dare not go to wash her.

    Which fear may be well-grounded; for any cow in China or elsewhere that has never been milked, is apt to be frightened by such an approach. 踢 TI², to kick; 踢人 TI² REN², kicks people; 不敢 BU² GAN³, not dare, I dare not.

已經喂過兩天，不怕得，該不得踢人

988 You have already fed her for two days; don't be afraid; she will probably not kick you.

    已經 I³ GIN¹, already; 不怕得 BU² PA⁴ DE² evidently a corruption of 不怕的 BU² PA⁴ DY², don't fear; 該不得 GAI¹ BU² DE², probably will not, ought not.

牛兒子拴來，挨倒大牛的腦殼

989 Tie the calf near the cow's head.

KEEPING A COW

哎呀,踢得兇,害怕

Ai ya! she kicks fiercely! I am afraid!

哎呀 AI³ YA², a common exclamatory expression; 兇 HSIUNG¹, fierce, fiercely.

喊老李揀一個瓦片,刮他的頸項

Call Lao Li to find a piece of broken tile, with which to scratch her neck.

揀 GIEN³, to find, to pick up, to select; 瓦片 WA³ PIEN³, a piece of broken tile; very commonly corrupted to WA³ PIER³; 刮 GWA², to scrape, to scratch; 頸項 GING³ HANG⁴, neck. The last is one of the few exceptions to the rule that words ending in *ing* drop the 'g' in West China.

還是不行

Still it won't work!

不行 BU² HSIN², a very common expression, best translated by some such expression as that given above, or 'it will not do', 'it cannot be worked', etc.

拿繩子來,把後脚拴來作攏

Bring a rope and tie her hind legs together.

繩子 SHWEN² DZ³, rope, cord, string. This word is just that much wider than 索子 SO² DZ³ which is pretty well restricted to 'rope'. 作攏 DZO² LUNG³, to bring together, brought together.

這下子，奶頭洗咯，跟倒擠奶子

994　Now then, wash her teats and proceed to milk her.

　　The word 把 BA³ is understood before 奶頭 LAI³ TOU². This is one more illustration of the tendency to brevity in ordinary speech, by omitting words.

擠得有幾杯奶子

995　How many cups of milk have you?

　　Lit., 'Squeezed obtained have how many cups milk?' 得 DE² is undoubtedly a corruption for 的 DY².

纔攎歸一，有十三杯

996　I have just finished measuring; there are thirteen cups.

　　攎 YIN⁴, to measure.

可以端進來濾

997　You may carry it in and strain it.

　　濾 LÜ⁴, to strain, whether through a cloth or a metal strainer. This word is often corrupted in speech to LI⁴, probably just because LI⁴ is easier to say than LÜ⁴.

濾奶子的帕子，濾一回洗一回

998　The cloth with which you strain the milk is to be washed every time you use it.

KEEPING A COW

Lit., 'Strain milk cloth, strain one time, wash one time'.

奶子濾過、倒在煑奶罐裏頭

999 When the milk has been strained, empty it into the milk-boiler.

'When' is understood, as 的時侯 DY² SHĪ² HOU⁴, after 過 GO⁴. 煑奶罐 DJU³ LAI³ GWAN⁴, milk-boiler; *lit.*, 'boil-milk-jug'.

用煑奶罐、把奶子坐開

1000 Bring the milk to a boil, using the milk-boiler.

Lit., 'Use milk-boiler, take milk, set boil'. 坐 DZO⁴, to set on the stove, or over the fire; 開 KAI¹, to open, to boil, to come to the boiling point.

回回用這個罐子、就不得把奶子煮煳

1001 You are to use this boiler every time, so that you will not burn the milk.

煳 FU², to scorch, to burn; 煮煳 DJU³ FU², to scorch in boiling.

奶子煑開了、就擱在涼快地方晾冷

1002 When the milk has boiled, you should place it in a cool place to cool.

'When' understood; 煑開 DJU³ KAI¹, to raise to the boiling point; 涼快 LIANG² KWAI⁴, cool; 晾冷 LIANG⁴ LEN³, to cool; *lit.*, to expose until cold.

出版后记

本书是一部 100 多年前加拿大人启尔德编写的学习四川话中英文对照教材。启尔德（Omar L. Kilborn 1867—1920），加拿大安大略省人，在金斯顿王后大学获得医学博士学位，1891 年自愿作为一名医学传教士前往中国，是最早一批来四川的外国人士。

启尔德在四川从事医疗卫生事业，为四川医疗的近代化作出了杰出贡献。1892 年，启尔德在成都东门的四圣祠街（今四圣祠北街）建立了四川地区第一家西式医院"福音医院"，却因语言不通，不到 3 个月就关闭了。启尔德积极参与筹建华西协合大学。1910 年华西协合大学正式开课，他成为学校理事会的第一任主席。1914 年华西协合大学医科建立后，启尔德又登上了讲台，讲授生理学、眼科和化学等课程。

这应该就是当年本书产生的历史背景。

启尔德对学习中文，特别是四川话有自己独特的理解，他认为迅速了解中国，听和说的能力尤为重要，其次是阅读中文的能力，再次就是书写中国汉字的能力。这四个过程对于刚学习中文的外国学生来说是相互联系、递进发展的，首先要掌握了听和说，才能更容易地学习汉字、阅读中文。

于是，他编写了一部方便来华外国人学习的方言教材。启尔德认为，学习四川话的精髓在于词汇和句子，而不是方块字本身，更不是成语。而面对来华如此繁重的工作，怎么选择所要学习的词汇和句子，达到事半功倍的效果呢？启尔德选取了很多四川人日常使用频率较高、相对简单的语言。比如，"先生这么早"（Good morning, Teacher）、"这个字读啥子"（How is this character pronounced?）……这些实用的短语和句子，可以想象是启尔德经过长期的积累总结起来的。

本书是百年前优秀的大学四川话英语教材，翻看它，仿佛时光穿梭，回到了民国那个充满传奇、新旧交错的时代，展现的是一段历史大幕下的东西文化交流、融合。

这也正是我们影印出版这本书的初衷。希望有更多的人和我们一起关注本土文化的历史和未来，让文化交融成为时代发展的推动力。

本书是根据收藏在加拿大多伦多大学图书馆的原件，即1917年由华西协合大学印刷出版的教材为底本，影印出版的。由于原件有很多不完美的地方，比如缺页、错别字、语法错误、油墨污点等，影印出版实在无法避免，敬请读者谅解。希望瑕不掩瑜，让更多的读者了解到这本书的价值。